MOVIE CHRISTS

and

ANTICHRISTS

Peter Malone

CROSSROAD • NEW YORK

1990

The Crossroad Publishing Company
370 Lexington Avenue, New York, NY 10017

Printed in the United States of America

Library of Congress Cataloging-in-Publication Data

Malone, Peter, 1954-
    Movie Christs and antichrists/Peter Malone.
        p.   cm.
    ISBN 0-8245-1003-8
    1. Jesus Christ in motion pictures.   2. Antichrist in motion
    pictures.   3. Redemption in motion pictures.   4. Evil in motion
    pictures.   I. Title.
    PN1995.9.J4M35   1990   89-37633
    791.43′651 — dc20   CIP

Acknowledgments
Quotations taken from the Jerusalem Bible published and © 1966, 1967 and
1968 by Darton, Longman and Todd Ltd. and Doubleday & Co. Inc. and used by
permission of the publishers.

The author wishes to thank the following:
Fr. Tony Doherty and John Devlin, for their enthusiasm about the project and
for making it happen.

Phyllis Coffey, for typing the manuscript.

Doug Baxter, Columbia Pictures Television, Sydney, for his assistance in
providing photographs.

Photographs: Front cover and text, used with the kind permission of the following: Columbia Pictures
Industries, Inc., pp. vi, 12, 32, 36, 44, 48, 60, 64, 68, 72, 84, 88, 108, 116, 120, 132, 136, 144, 152, 156; Goldcrest
Films and Television Ltd./CEL, p. 4; Goldcrest Distributors Ltd., pp. 96, 160; Edgar Rice Burroughs, Inc. and
Warner Bros. Inc., p. 8; Sharmill Films, p. 20; Hoyts Distribution Pty. Ltd., p. 24; Warner Bros., pp. 16, 56, 100;
Warner Bros. and Walter Selzer Productions, p. 40; Warner Bros. and Hoja Productions Inc., p. 124;
Inspirational Films, p. 28; De Laurentiis Entertainment Ltd., p. 52; CPT Holdings, Inc. and Columbia Pictures, p.
76; Filmpac Holdings Ltd., p. 80; The Ronin Films Group, p. 92; Embassy Film Associates/CEL, p. 104; Kennedy
Miller Productions Pty. Ltd., p. 112; Capital Cities/ABC Inc., p. 128; Brooksfilms/CEL, p. 140; Newvision Film
Distributors Pty. Ltd., p. 148; The Museum of Modern Art Film Stills Archive.

CONTENTS

GODSPELL . . . *The Gospel, the Good News, presented in song, dance and mime.*

A Religious Interpretation of Films

Watching a film can be enjoyable.
That's entertainment!
We know that films
can often be challenging.
They draw on our deepest feelings.
Christians sometimes recognise
the resemblances to the story of Jesus.
They identify Christ-figures.

Films — at the theatre, on television, on video — constitute a major 20th century entertainment form, and not just for affluent countries. Movies are seen world-wide. While looked at from differing cultural points of view, they can, nevertheless, be means of communication and unity in world culture. The goodies and baddies of the western (of the United States or whatever country) are universal characters.

George Lucas's **Star Wars** Force has been interpreted as Christian, as Buddhist and as satisfying a deep longing, by those who ignore or do not believe in a God, for meaning, value and power in life that is greater than the human.

It is amazing to some audiences how writers, teachers, reviewers, commentators declare that they can see resemblances, significant likenesses, between characters in films and Jesus Christ. There is the obvious danger of reading too much into a film. In the mediaeval epics popular in the '80s, like **Conan the Barbarian** or **The Sword and the Sorcerer,** the central character was crucified, was rescued or came back to life in some way. Christ-figures? Perhaps — although not everyone who suffers and stretches out arms is to be seen to resemble Jesus in a significant way.

But, allowing for a natural scepticism — something is not accepted until proven — it would be a pity if the important resemblances between film characters and Jesus were not noted and explored.

Film-makers sometimes make the comparisons deliberately. George Lucas has said this about Luke Skywalker. Melissa Mathison of **E.T.,** Mario Puzo of Superman in **Superman the Movie** and, at the other end of the movie business, European directors like Robert Bresson **(Au Hazard, Balthasar; Mouchette),** Luis Bunuel **(Nazarin; El)** and Ingmar Bergman **(Cries and Whispers)** have obviously intended their central characters to be responded to as Christ-figures.

While explicitly religious films have generally been popular through the decades, sometimes reverent **(King of Kings),** sometimes offbeat **(Jesus Christ, Superstar; Godspell),** the Christ-figures are not always in an explicitly 'religious' film. Something of both can be seen in what is considered one of the earliest full-length feature films, directed by the pioneer American film-maker D. W. Griffith in 1916: **Intolerance.** The screenplay interwove four stories on the theme of intolerance throughout the ages. One was the Judaean Story and it presented Jesus of Nazareth — at the wedding feast of Cana, with children, with the woman taken in adultery, before Pontius Pilate, Jesus crucified. The sequences were generally presented as tableaux; but Jesus himself was there, on the screen, a mixture of expected pious representation and a smiling, humane saviour.

There was also a Modern Story, however, with all the conventions that have since become stereotypes, even clichés: the poor boy finding city work, becoming involved with gangsters, framed, accused and tried for murder and narrowly saved from the gallows. Nothing new in the cinema! But his trial was intercut with the sequence of Jesus before Pilate. The editorial comment was obvious. The boy was to be seen in the perspective of the suffering of Jesus. He was presented as a Christ-figure. Thus in 1916, early days of feature films, we have what we might call a Jesus-figure (Jesus himself) and a Christ-figure (the boy).

Just over forty years later, something similar was done in the Oscar-winning spectacle **Ben Hur.** Early in the film Judah Ben Hur is in a slave-gang making its way north from Jerusalem. They stop at Nazareth. They are hot and sweating. A figure (although not shown fully, easily recognisable as Jesus) gives the slaves and Ben Hur some cool water. Later in the film, roles are reversed and as Jesus is seen on his Way of the Cross, it is Ben Hur who offers cool water to him. The novel's author, General Lew Wallace, called his book (and the film followed suit) 'A Tale of the Christ'. It is not difficult, therefore, to see Ben Hur as a Christ-figure.

The study of Christ-figures has become acceptable in connection with the novel, the play, the poem. In the 19th century, American authors like Herman Melville and Nathaniel Hawthorne wrote novels that were parables critical of their contemporaries whose religious principles were frequently founded on external respectability — that God blessed those who helped and blessed themselves. These authors challenged their readers with the biblical principle that man sees the face while God sees the heart.

Melville's **Billy Budd** was a character symbolic of innocence who was persecuted by the symbolic character of evil, Claggart. Hawthorne's Hester Prynne wore the scarlet letter 'A' for adulteress and was condemned and suffered in 17th century Salem, while the preacher-father of her child went undiscovered and respectable. This religious study of literature is valid. The story of Jesus is such a part of European and western culture that its significance has influenced and has been used by the great writers and dramatists.

The same is true of film-makers. It is time to respond to these images and themes when we find them. ■

THE KILLING FIELDS . . . *Dr. Haing S. Ngor as Dith Pran, who suffers in Cambodian prison camps, and Sam Waterston as journalist Sydney Schanberg, in an emotion-charged episode.*

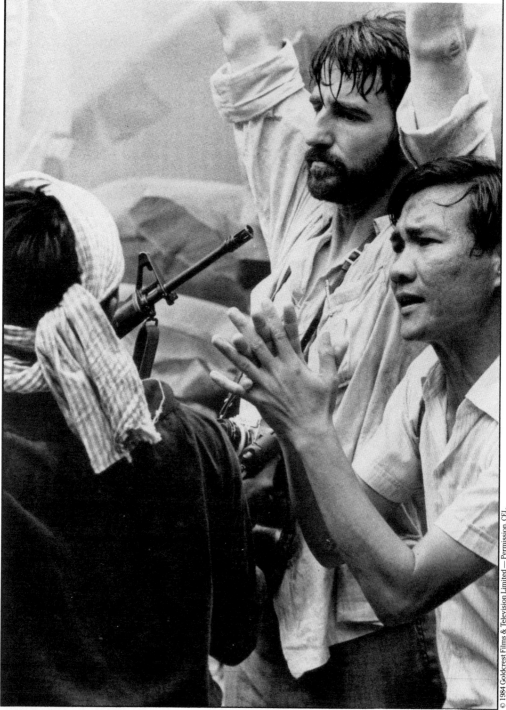

Film-makers: Their Art and Challenge

Film has its particular impact on audiences.
They respond to images rather than to words
(the heritage of recent centuries).
They respond to the creative devices
of shaping and linking these moving images.

We look at the effect of films on ourselves and the technical skill that has gone into making them. After all, this experiential approach is how we all encountered films. We have watched them for years before our first lesson on cinema techniques.

An interesting way of considering response and technique is to contrast our response to looking at words and to looking at images. Our sight is the principal sense in reading (although we can follow the line with our finger). But, even though the eye is used, its function is mainly mechanical unless an artist has laid out a page with some care. The words are merely signs and the imagination has to take over and provide the material for our minds and understanding to work on. If we grasp the words, if our imaginations are activated and we understand, then we can get emotionally involved in what we read.

The development of the process runs: sense experience, initial intellectual grasp, imaginative response, emotional response, intellectual understanding and evaluation.

When we respond to moving images, the process is different. We certainly use our eyes at once (and, with sound films, our ears) but the images are not merely conventional signs of communication. Design, colour, movement, rhythms are all presented at once to us. And at once we respond on the level of pleasurable or unpleasurable sense and emotional response. Our primary, or initial, intellectual grasp coincides with this vivid sensory and emotional response.

The imagination does not have to work as hard as it does in reading, because images are provided to the senses. But the imagination is at work nonetheless, along with emotions, as regards identification with or rejection of the reality presented by the images. It is on this personal response process that intellectual understanding is based.

The development of the process runs: sensory experience, emotional response, initial intellectual grasp, imaginative collaboration, intellectual understanding and evaluation.

The difference between responding to words and responding to images lies, first of all, in the immediate sense response. There is so much more demand made on us at once in response to images: senses and emotions. The personal involvement is so much greater. The impact should be so much more forceful than words which are read. Since the emotions are involved immediately with our senses, the imaginative collaboration is also felt more emotionally.

The value of reading is that so much demand is made on our concentration that the work of the imagination is much more intense; we put more of ourselves, perhaps, into our imaginative response which then calls for our emotions to join in. Ultimately, both experiences bring forth insight and understanding, but the interplay of senses, emotions and imagination is where the differences lie.

To appreciate the particular creativity of film, we need to remember the scientific and technical developments of the 19th century: film stock, cameras, film projectors. The developments of the 20th century have been particularly sophisticated. The second half of the 20th century has seen enormous technical developments in sizes of screen, lenses, special effects and stunts for cinematic power.

One way of realising how films work is to look at a comic strip. We can note the way the cartoonist has set a perspective in each frame of his strip. If each panel was similar (e.g. heads of talking people), it would become boring. However, there are close-ups of heads and faces, perhaps some extreme close-ups of an eye or an ear; there are medium shots of cars on a road and long shots of a whole view of a city.

It is not difficult (perhaps while watching television commercials!) to learn to classify the different kinds of shots. One can soon become alert to their use and effectiveness.

Since films are not mere comics but are moving images, there is a complexity in the presentation of the types of shot. One can learn how moving shots are taken: e.g. whether the camera is on a tripod and swivels round, 'panning'; or whether the camera tilts up and down. Sometimes, as in a riding scene in a western, the camera is moved along beside the horse and rider and 'tracks' its subject. Even in a room, a camera can track back and forth. To move, especially in outdoor scenes, the camera can move from medium to long shots on a crane.

The lens of the camera itself can be used in different ways. Focal length might be suddenly changed and, from a long shot, one can suddenly 'zoom' into a close-up and out again. One can focus attention on a person who is close and blur the background and then reverse it. Once again television commercials can offer an easily accessible 'text' to note how filming is done.

The possibilities of lighting and composition within each shot, whether it be panning or tilting or a zoom, give enormous scope for a film-maker to experiment not only on what his film looks like, but how it works on an audience: the difference between using close-up and medium shot, between a speedy zoom or a smooth slow panning — the pace, rhythm, mood of film depend on this.

But if something is not satisfying in the shots, there is still a creative area of film-making that might remedy it or enhance it: joining the shots — editing.

In home movies, each sequence is more or less tacked onto the next. This may be one reason why they are so dull for everyone except the family cavorting in them. Ingenuity in joining the shots, improving them, playing with their impact on audiences, seeing the possibilities of manipulation, these are part of the creativity of editing.

Some techniques are familiar to us: fade-ins and fade-outs, slow dissolves, quick cross-cutting, superimposition, juxtaposing shots of the same person or situation from different angles. Skill in editing, estimating the appropriate rhythms for a film, utilising the best material available for all the celluloid exposed, is an important field of this creativity.

We have so far concentrated on visual creativity which is of primary importance. The quality of the soundtrack, whether it is to be 'realistic' (simply using the sounds that were recorded) or whether the sounds must be eliminated and others dubbed in, where the voices of commentators have to be edited with the images, whether the actors' words have to be post-synchronised with their images on the screen (as has to be done with animated films), how the musical score is to be joined to the film — these are all further areas of editing creativity.

These elements all contribute to the appreciation of the art of film. ■

GREYSTOKE . . . *Popular hero Tarzan, Lord of the Apes (Christophe Lambert) gets lavish treatment in this film version of the legend.*

3

A Question of Values

While an appreciation of techniques
enhances the response to a film,
it is the content
that draws the response from the audience.
Content leads us to consider
the values underlying it —
both what is presented and how it is presented.

Considerations and our response to films and alertness to techniques lead us to the **content** of a film, its meaning.

Audiences know that they like a plot, some coherence (not necessarily step-by-step logic) and some resolution of issues, even if the resolution is somewhat indeterminate. Some semblance of narrative is generally required and some presentation of recognisable values, no matter how sketchy or superficial.

All art, no matter what techniques are used to communicate and to draw response from the audience, presents and probes some human values. A clever political cartoon, a painted portrait, an abstract sculpture, a beautiful building, all are the work of insight, human dignity and are part of human vision. Novels and plays probe the human situation, mirroring nature in a heightened realism or a stylised impressionism, freeing our feelings and emotions in the response they ask for.

In tragedy, human flaws and mistakes and their consequences are probed, often to show human insight into self through suffering. In comedy, we are cut down to size or, rather, seen at the right size, neither super-heroic nor insignificant, but funny creatures of foibles, whims and lovability.

Romance, melodrama, historical pageant, adventure — these all, in their own way, have as their content, human values.

To check this, without being over-serious about it and imputing greater depths of human understanding to some average commercial director of standard westerns, for instance, we can look at feature films and the basic values they believe in or are actually promoting: why, on its own level of values, a film appeals to an audience. Along with this kind of estimating of a film's theme, we can also estimate whether human values are being skipped over or rubbished.

On the level of values, the film engages audience attention because of its probing of what it is to live, to be, to die or to survive. Questions of identity, what it is to be a person, what it is to exist, are fundamental to us all, and films that present and examine this theme are vital to us.

Often we feel that we can never find all the answers to life's problems. Yet, somehow or other, our feelings, our experience and our ideas tell us that solutions to problems are often more possible than we might at first realise: that the mystery of life is inexhaustible but that it can be penetrated more and more.

There is always more. We can always understand this more and we should never give up or opt out. This basic drive in us to something outside ourselves (or, for many, some**one** outside themselves) is a drive for humanity to transcend itself. There are so many of what have been called 'signals of transcendence' alerting us to move outside ourselves and to seek whatever harmony there is in the universe and to see how it outweighs the disharmony.

There have been many pessimistic films which invite an audience concerned about values to identify emotionally with a disillusioned character — to experience the need for harmony and peace which they cannot find or find only in the despairing surrender of death. The harmony that could be ours is frequently seen more vividly in its absence than its presence. No answers may emerge from the film itself but questions of value have been more strongly asked and more deeply understood.

Thus, in saying that human values are the content of a film (and that the unique way they come to the audience is by skilfully arranged moving images rather than through words, plaster or paint) we are pinpointing basic human drives:

the drive to live,
the drive to love,
the drive to live socially,
the drive to transcend self.

If these are incorporated into a film, then they make corresponding demands on an audience. The experience of a film can be a real growth in human awareness.

One could call this experience 'education' — education in the broadest sense of the word. A good film can, if we let it, draw us out of ourselves to our better, more aware selves. And this is not too much different from genuine entertainment, which is not just a laugh, a thrill or a giggle but something which really satisfies us personally. We are the better (our better selves) for it.

This closeness of true education and true entertainment could be a lead for solving some of the difficulties of people who are wary of films which look too serious and who retreat from them with 'I like a film to be entertaining'. A wholly entertaining film is **energy-restoring** rather than **debilitatingly escapist.**

A difficulty facing many film-goers, as well as audiences confronted by documentaries, short films or experimental material, is that they are not sure what kind of film is being screened for them. Audiences are still not able to recognise readily the type of film before them, its particular **genre.**

Each genre has its own conventions — these conventions are actually often recognised, but audiences do not make sufficient allowance for recognising the genre. This means that audiences tend to take many films literally or merely at what seems to be face value. Realism can be recognised but subtleties go by unnoticed.

Learning to recognise and appreciate different genres of film, their particular styles and conventions, will help audiences become more 'visuate' — able to appreciate what they see.

One of the major consequences of not understanding genres is that audiences find it hard to grasp what values are being probed or presented in the film or whether there are any.

Audiences deserve the opportunity to become aware of or train themselves to appreciate the genres of films and recognise conventions. They will then realise the intelligence and imagination behind a film's conception and execution, the use of techniques within the genre, and the characterisations and plot-complexities within the context of the whole film. Prominent and recognisable genres include, of course: love story, drama, thriller, western, comedy, musical, war film, mystery, science-fiction, historical spectacle, religious film.

This approach to the whole film, its context, and its consistency of values of good and bad within this context, is a necessary basis for the moral assessment made of films by parents, churchmen or civic leaders, especially censors. Looking at sequences and situations within the film gives a sounder basis for assessing the moral worth of the film, rather than a method which simply labels or categorises the content of a film almost without feeling the need for seeing it, and condemns or approves accordingly. Murder and adultery are bad; religion and patriotism are good, without a consideration of the quality of the complete film.

One needs to remember that the complete film is not over until the last scene fades from the screen.

These points indicate how important it is when assessing the content of a film and its values to make the distinction between **What** the film is presenting and **How** it is being presented. Basically, anything human can be presented as regards the **What.** Subtlety, differing perspectives (and even controversy) enter with the **How.** ■

STARMAN . . . *Jeff Bridges received an Oscar nomination for his role as the kindly alien. With Karen Allen.*

4

Film and the Storyteller's World

Stories take us into their world.
The more successful the storytelling,
the better we identify with this world,
its situations, events
and, of course, its characters.
But the variety of ways of storytelling
means that we can have different responses
to the world we enter.

Storytelling is older than writing. The tale told by the human storyteller is better because of the qualities of voice, modulation, pauses, excitement, sadness and laughter that the storyteller brings to the stories. Poetry, its rhythms and melodies, a range of lyrics, songs, ritual refrains and choruses, have shaped stories and their worlds for centuries, indeed for millenia. The age-old types of storytelling have been developed and sophisticated. Identifying them and their approaches to the world they make, helps us in appreciating how Christ-figures are used.

A film generally catches our imaginations, our feelings, and enables us to move to insights. It takes us into its own world. It may be the 'realistic' world of **Godfather** films or of **Ordinary People,** a nostalgic past like that of **Chariots of Fire** or a fantasy future of empires, wars and Jedi.

One writer offers the following schema for considering stories and the world they make:

Parable   : subverts world
Satire   : attacks world
Action   : investigates world
Apologue : defends world
Myth   : establishes world

Each of these can be considered in turn.

Parable. One way a film invites us into its world is by portraying a story that lures us but then disturbs us. We recognise this kind of a film as a parable. What happens in parable is often the opposite of what the audience expects. Needless to say, too diagrammatic an application of the theory is not possible, especially as the stories become more complex. Jesus, a shrewd educator by parables, stayed with brevity and comparative straightforwardness.

Carson McCuller's moving story of a deaf mute, **The Heart is a Lonely Hunter,** is a Christ-figure parable. Set in the American South, it is the story of John Singer. A loner, he takes on the responsibility for a retarded friend, another deaf-mute, who has to be hospitalised. Mr Singer moves to the town where his friend is and boards with a family who need the rental money to help support themselves. The father has been incapacitated in an accident and the mother has to manage and bring up their 16-year-old daughter, Mick, and her young brothers. John Singer encounters a number of people in the town: Mick, a drunken vagrant, a negro doctor, his rebellious daughter and her husband. In his own way, he changes their lives.

The film ends tragically. The burden is too great for him and he shoots himself, uniting his friends by his death. A jolting, sad parable.

Satire. This is a 'black' form of storytelling. Of set purpose, the satirist is negative. A caustic moralist, the satirist knows that the real world should be better than it is. Since it is not, he picks the faults, the abuses, the sins, and holds them up to the light but then mocks, invites his audience to laugh at them. Some audiences take everything at what they think is face value, interpreting satire too literally, and are offended. The satirist wants to offend those who subscribe to the follies, or abuses being attacked, but implies that there are positive values that he believes in.

The original **M*A*S*H, Catch 22** satirised war. **Bedazzled** satirised human pride, ambitions and failure and foibles. The Monty Python group has satirised everything from funny walks and the Middle Ages to **The Meaning of Life.** Their attack on biblical spectacles, religious fanaticism, unions and Women's Liberation, **The Life of Brian,** offers a satiric Christ-figure.

Action. This kind of story is the easiest to respond to. It describes a world and investigates it. Most popular entertainment fits into this category: from the basic narratives of situation-comedy or soap-opera to the dramas that mirror the concerns of contemporary society. While the world of the action story has its own inner coherence as well as its boundaries, it is readily entered into for acceptance or rejection by large audiences.

Charlton Heston is noted for roles such as Moses, Ben Hur, Michelangelo, General Gordon, Richelieu, El Cid etc., etc. He was also a Christ-figure in a lesser known action science-fiction feature about the end of the world, **The Omega Man** (suggestive title in itself). After trying to save the survivors of nuclear catastrophe and fight the evil radioactive spectres, he dies, his heart pierced, his blood flowing into a water-fountain.

Apologue. Apologue is an off-putting term, especially in comparison with the others. Yet from the point of view of traditional terminology, it has some merit. An old word, 'Apologetics', was used in a religious context. It has been understood always as the explanation and defence of faith. In the 19th century Cardinal Newman used the Latin term for his religious autobiography, Apologia Pro Vita Sua (An Apologue for His Life). Taking the key ideas 'explanation' and 'defence', we can say that an apologue is a story that offers its audience a world that promotes itself, by explaining or defending itself.

Many explicitly religious films can be seen as apologues. Films which present priests and nuns, for instance, doing much needed social work tend to dramatise and hallow them. Spencer Tracy won an Oscar in the '30s for his role as Father Flanagan, the founder of Boys' Town. **Boys' Town** and the many similar films show us a world that the film-makers say they believe in and invite audiences to believe in as well.

Myth. Myth is seen to be, with parable, the most important kind of story. Myth is the profound and positive story. It creates world. It creates world in the sense that the story can use, for plot and characters, real/historical personages or fictitious persons and tell a story where meaning is the important thing. Thus in the classic literature of cultures and religions there are 'myths' that are the means for getting in touch with and communicating the spiritual meaning of the culture and religion.

The creation and development of myths has been influenced at times by oral traditions, literary forms and popular modes of storytelling. There is no reason why 20th century cinema styles and ways of communicating cannot shape new myths or reshape old myths. The **Star Wars** and **Superman** films have been obvious examples of '70s and '80s popular myths.

Going back to literature for an example of a version of myth, we can consider a novel that has been filmed at least three times, Charles Dickens' **A Tale of Two Cities.** Set at a crucial time of European history, highlighting the contrast between 18th century English and French societies, the story was written originally for readers in Victorian England and the expanding British Empire. Beneath the details of the tale, however, is a universal story — people in danger and loving one another are saved. Sidney Carton, seemingly a man of few values, shows himself a man of principle and lays down his life in a violent death so that others may live.

It is clearly a variation on the story of Jesus' death — the greatest love is the laying down of life for friends. Dickens (and the film versions dramatise this) knew that this plot is an ideal, a story that gives some spiritual meaning to life. And this is myth. ■

PALE RIDER . . . *A girl prays the 'Our Father' and Clint Eastwood arrives as an apocalyptic avenger.*

5

A Key Distinction: Jesus-figures and Christ-figures

We can use the terms,
Jesus-figure and Christ-figure.
The Jesus-figure refers specifically
to portrayals of Jesus himself.
The Christ-figure is anyone else
who is made to resemble Jesus
in a significant and substantial way,
as a redeemer-figure or a saviour-figure.

There is an immediate distinction to be made between Jesus-figures and Christ-figures. The lead was given by Malachi Martin in his entertainingly instructive book **Jesus Now.** He himself was particularly interested in the variations in Jesus-figures over the centuries and how art, religion and popular piety were influenced by historical and social conditions.

● The Jesus-figure is any representation of Jesus himself.

● The Christ-figure is a character (from history, fiction, visual arts, poetry, drama, music, cinema) who is presented as resembling Jesus in a significant way.

The Jesus-figure can be presented in a 'realistic' way or in a 'stylised' way.

Realistic: Jesus as he was thought to be.

● One of the main difficulties of this kind of presentation of Jesus is that it has tended and still tends to be based on a fundamentalist interpretation of Scripture — the reading of Scripture as if written solely for the reader's present rather than looking at it with the mentality of the time of the writer. This requires some knowledge of the Old Testament background and of biblical literary forms.

● Cinema 'realistic' presentation tends to rely on the well-known or classic visual portraits of Jesus.

● These presentations have tended to soften Jesus. It was Marxist Italian director Pier Paolo Pasolini who attempted to portray a rugged Jesus in the mid-'60s in his **Gospel According to Matthew.**

● Most 'realistic' portraits are, in fact, quite stylised. Have we any real picture of Jesus 'as he was'?

● The more closely the portrait of Jesus is based on a 'scientific-spiritual' reading of the Gospels, the more realistic it will be. Franco Zeffirelli with his **Jesus of Nazareth** has come closest so far.

Stylised: Jesus presented in contemporary or in deliberately 'unrealistic' settings.

• This happened immediately in the early Christian centuries with Jesus linked to the styles of Greek or Roman art as well as with politics — the Jesus All-Powerful of the Ravenna mosaics.

• We are used to seeing Jesus in Italian settings in Mediaeval and Renaissance art; or listening to Handel's or Bach's sacred scores e.g. of Jesus' Passion.

• Though originally surprising or shocking, the stylistic presentations of Jesus visually and in music, **Jesus Christ, Superstar** and **Godspell** are now taken for granted.

• Artists will continue to surprise, delight or shock — from Aboriginal Madonna and Child to Georges Rouault's clown-like Jesus, to Stanley Kubrick's **A Clockwork Orange,** where Alex has fantasies about Jesus — that he is participating in Jesus' passion, whipping him and making him suffer.

Many find the immediate impact of these figures too contrived, but they continue a respected art tradition where Jesus is placed in the art styles of the times.

The Christ-figure, it is suggested, can be a redeemer-figure or a saviour-figure. These categories are not mutually exclusive. The particular focus of each is what is emphasised.

Redeemer-figures — representing Jesus taking on human burdens and sinfulness in suffering, even death.

Saviour-figures — representing Jesus' saving mission, even to triumph and resurrection.

Particular focuses on Christ lead to a variety of redeemer and saviour-figures:

• Martyr-figures: suffering and death as a witness to values and convictions.

• Job-like figures: innocent sufferers, the persecuted.

• Popular saviours: legendary knights or contemporary pop-heroes.

• Clown-figures: highlighting the fact that God's folly is wiser than human wisdom.

• Community-builders: reconciling and bringing people together.

• Growth stages: reminding us that human growth is in developmental stages.

• Off-beat figures: not only human beings but Watership rabbits and Tolkien Hobbits.

• Mad saviours: the various Don Quixotes with saving ideals and convictions.

• Satiric figures: religiosity and 'piousness' can be laughed at.

Tradition has offered men as Christ-figures. But women saints from Mary and Gospel times to the present have shown the feminine Christ-figure. Ingmar Bergman in **Cries and Whispers** shows how a cinema artist can offer a moving and significant feminine redeemer-figure.

Traditional figures include messengers from God, often 'angels', saints, priests and nuns.

The pattern of Jesus' life is a universal pattern seen in the lives of significant figures not in the Judaeo-Christian tradition, for instance the Buddha or Gandhi. One can ask whether it is appropriate to refer to them as Christ-figures.

In a world of evil and sinfulness, there have always been personifications of evil. The New Testament uses the word 'antichrist'. Considerations of Christ-figures must include consideration of antichrist-figures. ■

CAMMINA, CAMMINA . . . 'Keep on Walking' is the English title of the biblical film in which Ermanno Olmi made the Infancy Narratives quite Italian.

6

Film as Religious Art

*There is a long tradition of Christian art
providing many styles for representing Christ.
While 19th century piety influenced directors,
20th century variety offers creative possibilities
to film-makers.*

Cinema is a 20th century art form, a combination of technology and creativity: machines, lenses, film stock and the variety of shapes, sizes, designs, colours in edited moving images. However, while the experimental skills of 20th century art and design have shaped the style of cinema, when religious themes are presented or indicated, the images of the past combine with those of the present for religious iconography.

There is a tradition of strength and beauty in the visual portrayal of Jesus.

• Jesus 'orante' — the praying Jesus of early frescoes. Jewish tradition did not encourage visual representation of God so there was no direct artistic influence on early Christian art. Rather, contemporary Roman styles (e.g. frescoes at Pompeii, mosaics, sarcophagi carvings, vessels in the Vatican Necropolis) were adapted. Many of the symbols were adapted, 'baptised', e.g. the peacock and paradisiacal afterlife, the phoenix and its resurrection from the ashes.

Symbols and inscriptions e.g. the ICHTHUS fish symbol, Alpha and Omega, the cross.

• Jesus in the mysteries of the New Testament: catacomb frescoes of the nativity, cures, the Last Supper (and e.g. Jonah as a Christ-figure of the risen Jesus). Jesus as Teacher, Wonder-Worker, Son.

• The Risen Jesus, Judging, Ascending, Shepherd. Jesus' suffering is not so dominant in early art; perhaps the experience of persecution and the Acts of the Martyrs supplied for this. The crucified Jesus is a man more of serenity than of suffering, e.g. the priestly Jesus on the cross in a fresco in the Roman Forum.

• Jesus Pantocrator: the all-powerful Jesus, especially of the Ravenna and Venice Basilica mosaics with their glitter and their grandeur. These mosaics still last. They echo the styles of the Roman emperor's court — this-worldly and other-worldly.

• Jesus 'Monk': the presentation and symbolising of Jesus in the monastery manuscripts, e.g. the Irish book of Kells.

• Jesus Human/Spiritual — in the stained-glass windows, the cribs, the crucifixes of the mediaeval period. This is echoed in the development of the mysteries of the Rosary.

• Jesus Human: the artistic splendour of the Renaissance from Raphael to

Michelangelo, large canvases and frescoes, art often for reputation's sake and not necessarily religious. Yet this art is powerful and splendid.

There were many variations on this by such idiosyncratic and pessimistic visionaries as Bruegel and Bosch.

• The more passionate Jesus of the Baroque period. After technical expertise and achievement in the Renaissance, the heightening grandiosity of 17th century art. The humanity of Jesus was expressed in the devotion (often anti-Jansenistic) of the times, e.g. the origins of devotions to and images of the Sacred Heart.

The more balanced and warm spirituality of Vincent de Paul and Francis de Sales, with 'the interior sentiments of Jesus' echoed in such art as that of Rembrandt.

• The Romantic reaction of the 19th century against too much 18th century reason and enlightenment — yet the widespread impoverishment of taste and style: the strength of devotions, yet the sentimentality of holy card art. The emphasis on 'the pious' (even a Victorian image with Holman Hunt's pre-Raphaelite Jesus the Light knocking on the door, in St. Paul's Cathedral, London).

• Developments in modern art were not particularly religious. However, greater creativity and experimentation renewed perceptions of Georges Rouault, Salvador Dali.

• The 'renewal' of the second part of the 20th century has meant the broadest range of representations of Jesus — many of which will be eventually spurned and used to label a partial sensibility which may need to be reacted against. An emphasis on the human, realistic Jesus (even the popularity amongst the young of Jesus Surfie!). Also a development in stylised representation — the ethnic as well as abstract styles.

Attempts at modern Jesus-figures and symbols may be seen in Coventry Cathedral and its furnishings and decoration.

While the cinema developed alongside the last two periods mentioned and presents them in documentary and animation, there is little evidence in feature films except in eccentric directors like Ken Russell and Federico Fellini.

The iconography of Cecil B. De Mille and the '60s Jesus movies is over-reverent homage to the classics or acceptance of the sentimental, popular 19th century style, some of which can be labelled kitsch. This was confirmed by the tendency to use lighting for halo or visionary impact. Heavenly choirs (rather than earthy or earthly choirs) and baroque orchestrations accompanied this iconography to inflated effect.

Healthy reaction came from Pier Paolo Pasolini whose black and white rugged young Jesus (according to Matthew) appealed to 20th century sensibilities, and Franco Zeffirelli in **Jesus of Nazareth** who used the classics in the same sensitive and respectful way that he filmed Shakespeare and opera. As a variation on a biblical score, he used devices like the pharisee Nicodemus reciting on the soundtrack the Fourth Servant Song from Isaiah, the song of suffering, as Jesus carried his cross to Calvary. With Laurence Olivier as Nicodemus, the quality recitation matched the images.

Veteran French director Marcel Carne chose to use only iconography for his version of **The Bible.** Relying on the landscapes of Sicily and the frescoes in its churches, he used camera movement, editing and sound to create a cinema impression of the Old Testament and of the life of Jesus. His research into the language and literature of the Bible was too literal, too fundamentalist, but he showed possibilities for cinema images of the Bible.

An image immediately recognisable for Christian iconography is the cross, the sign of the cross, or the church, especially steeples. Crosses and churches are used for quick signs rather than as symbols.

At the opening of the 1959 expose of brittle Italian society, **La Dolce Vita,** the audience is treated to the surrealistic experience of a large statue of Jesus being carried, often swaying, by helicopter over the city of Rome, an ironic conception of Christ over the eternal city which had lost faith in him. Director Federico Fellini, admirer of the music hall and the circus, and fascinated by the beauty and ugliness of the grotesque, is an example of the director who goes back again and again to his religious heritage to remember, to mock, to regret, to criticise, to exorcise the past.

In his **Juliet of the Spirits,** the heroine relives in a ghoulish memory psycho-drama the school-play where she portrayed a virgin martyr. Fellini, like Ken Russell, has a cinematic flair for new religious iconography that can be both creative and offensive.

While film-makers have relied on images from the past — and the tradition must be respected — they must now picture Jesus-figures for 20th century sensibilities. ■

ANNIE'S COMING OUT . . . *A true story, both factual and symbolic, of love and healing; with Tina Arhondis and Angela Punch-McGregor.*

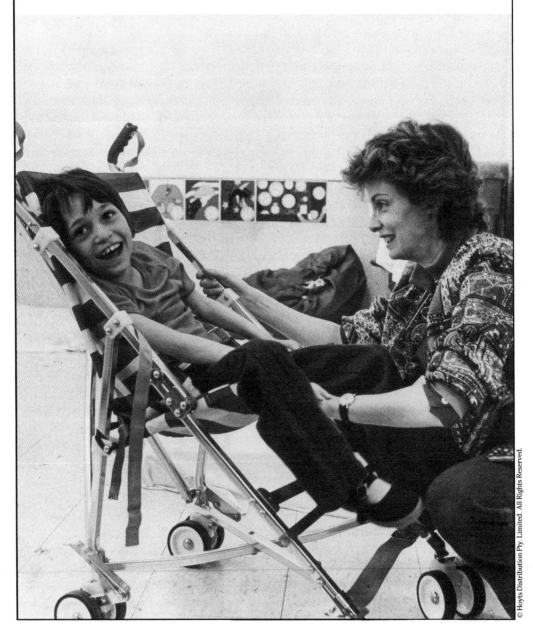

7

Signs and Symbols

*Images delight us and can draw us
into the richness of their meaning.
They can be signs, indicators,
leading us to other realities;
or they can be symbols,
inviting us into their own reality.*

What has been taken for granted in art study and was a feature of reflection on Old and New Testaments in the early church and in the Middle Ages especially, is now an important subject in the study of philosophy and theology: symbols. The distinction at once brought up is that between sign and symbol.

A sign is a means of pointing the way to something. We have distances and directions on signposts. We have internationally-known diagrams to indicate road hazards for traffic. We have ways of greeting. We have printing codes to indicate emphases for type-setting.

Signs are an efficient and an effective way of communicating information. It is often remarked that signs in general do not draw attention to themselves, make no demands of us of themselves. They indicate, point out, what we are to do or not do.

In terms of Christian iconography in films, there are several universally-known signs. Film-makers often include them for conveying quick information: a sign of the cross to indicate Catholic belief, a crucifix to indicate the Christianity of a particular people in a particular location. Churches are used as landmarks and to indicate traditional Christian practices: baptisms, marriages and funerals. The same is true of heavenly choir style music.

The screenwriter does not want the audience to spend any time responding to the sign itself. The sign is just a means for information. Any extra dimension is that of piety or devotion.

It is interesting (perhaps disturbing) to note the use of the name of God and of Jesus Christ so frequently as an expletive. Christians are offended. The expletives ignore the sensitivities of committed believers. However, linguistically, the use of these names means that they are significant enough to be used to vent anger or amazement. The words function mainly as signs — of the feelings expressed by the swearers. They do not ask for any real awareness of or insight into God or the person of Jesus Christ.

The acceptability of such usage is indicated by ever-changing community standards. The church has always used the Second Commandment language to describe this. It is not blasphemy, but taking the Lord's name in vain.

Psychologists have alerted us to the range of symbols. We consider art, ancient and new, and find recurring images and motifs. People recount their dreams and discover the same images. They are so frequently associated with religious teaching or ritual that it is appropriate to speak of religious symbolism.

The depth of meaning in the realm and experience of symbol is important for religious experience and is considered as basic for appreciating the sacraments. In 'The Book of Sacramental Basics', Tad Guzie notes:

> The profoundness of a symbol lies in its being just what it is. Giving or receiving a gift, sharing a meal, laying hands on a friend in love or blessing are profound things. A symbol is its own reality, and **in** its own reality it leads us into the profound mystery which it signifies. If a symbol is worth its name, it is so expressive of the familiar mystery which it signifies that it could never be called "only a symbol." If there were such a thing, why should we get angry when someone burns our country's flag? ... The wedding rings that my wife and I wear are the same gold bands that my grandparents wore. If they were lost, and if they are "only symbols," why should we be upset at anything more than the high price of gold?
>
> All true symbols shape our reality. When a symbol is brought forward or enacted, reality is altered for us. **All true symbols are efficacious.** In the very act of signifying a reality, they both make and change our reality. (p.50)

In recent decades it has become easier to talk about Jesus himself as a symbol. John's Gospel is particularly strong in this theme. Jesus often speaks of his oneness with his Father and of his showing his Father's 'glory' in what he said and did, especially in his dying. He told Thomas that he was the very Way, Truth and Life. He also reassured Philip that whoever saw (experienced) him saw (experienced) the Father.

In considering the long tradition of the church in talking of Jesus as one person, but with a divine nature and a human nature, we realise that his disciples directly experienced his humanity, a warm, appreciative and humane Jesus. Jesus' experience was **heart**felt and we speak of the very heart (not the language of physiology but of the person) as a symbol of Jesus. The traditions of art and iconography have explored and developed ways in which these symbols are portrayed and evoked.

Jesus-figures and Christ-figures can be considered symbolic. Of course, they have their limitations — of insight or of taste. But, as we experience them, they 'tip us into a new reality'. There is added experience of the reality of Jesus, added meaning.

The image of Vincent de Paul taking the place of a galley slave illuminates Jesus' laying down of life for friends. Some of the lyrics of **Jesus Christ, Superstar** sounded strange, brash or offensive in 1970. Yet the rock opera has elicited new awareness of Jesus' humanity, friendship, betrayal, hurt, agony. Even the crucifix talking to Don Camillo combines the reverent regard for Jesus Redeemer and the down-to-earth, humorous reassurance of his spiritual common-sense.

Writers, directors, actors and actresses are symbol-discoverers, symbol-makers. Guzie reminds us:

A real symbol always brings us into touch not just with a memory but with a living present, and indeed a present which contains a hope for the future and which helps to carry us into the future. (p.49) ■

JESUS . . . *Brian Deacon stars in this devout, too literal presentation of Luke's Gospel.*

8

Realistic Jesus-figures

Jesus himself has been portrayed regularly
on the 20th century screen.
Most portrayals have attempted
to present Jesus 'realistically',
to present Jesus 'as he was'.

The first film-makers were influenced by the traditional pictures of Jesus. With almost 2000 years of visual art heritage, including the work of such artists as the mosaic workers of Ravenna, Giotto in the Middle Ages and the great Renaissance fresco painters, it seems a pity that the popular styles of the late 19th century found their way to the screens and have tended to form popular audience taste. These styles are those of the old holy cards or statues which tend to be very pious, artificially coloured and rather 'sweet'. They are not considered to be very good art. In fact, many label them as kitsch art.

D. W. Griffith in **Intolerance** and Cecil B. De Mille in his 1923 **The King of Kings** were very influential in setting this holy card style as the norm for screen presentations of Jesus. However, this kind of representation was not restricted to American film-makers. In 1899 the Salvation Army made some films and slides for an evening's instructive programme, **Soldiers of the Cross,** for use in Melbourne. 19th century styles were influential. Films from Europe focusing on Jesus and made in the silent era have a similar iconography.

The main difficulty with this kind of interpretation of Jesus is that the Gospels themselves were read according to the principles of fundamentalist movements, a 20th century literalness, rather than going back to the mind of the first century A.D. The fundamentalist has little knowledge of the literary forms of the Old Testament and the New and so is unable to perceive the full message of the Gospel as it was presented in its time. The consequent Jesus-figure, therefore, is that of the popular sermon, the heartfelt prayer and mass-produced statuary and holy cards. At its best, it could be called devotional.

This style was reinforced by the techniques of the silent film. Since Jesus was not heard speaking and, since the acting style (derived from stage techniques) was that of the large gesture, the intense eye movement, the exaggerated posture, the Jesus-figure on the screen was larger than life, often an animated statue with a decidedly other-worldly fervour and sanctity. The caption cards with a tendency towards archaic language also emphasised this. Soon the orchestrated epic music was to reinforce it.

Jesus was to be reverenced. He did not make many explicit appearances during the '30s, '40s and '50s. His presence was rather suggested. He was glimpsed from a distance, or perceived by his effect on heroes and heroines, especially converts and penitents. This was emphasised as they began to be surrounded by halo light and lift their eyes to heaven.

Preston Foster as a gladiator-blacksmith hero dying in the 1935 **Last Days of Pompeii** was a case in point. Victor Mature was at the foot of the cross in the 1953 **The Robe.** At the end of this film Jean Simmons and Richard Burton, martyred and marching heavenwards to celestial choruses in the first Cinemascope production, are popular examples of this kind of effect of Jesus on the screen.

These films were successful at the box office, not received well critically and, in kinder retrospect, are said to be the products of their times.

While the 1959 **Ben Hur** (called 'A Story of the Christ') had glimpses of Jesus, there was the imaginative and Gospel-inspired parallel in Jesus giving Ben Hur water in Nazareth and the courtesy being returned on Jesus' way to Calvary. The 1962 **Barabbas** (literally 'son of the father') made some interesting parallels of the robber with Jesus, the Son of the Father. While the Gospels still tended to be read in the fundamentalist, 20th century literal way, Jesus in the '60s was seen to be portrayed by such actors as the youthful Jeffrey Hunter in **The King of Kings** and the rather dour Max von Sydow in **The Greatest Story Ever Told.**

Pier Paolo Pasolini is frequently praised for his black-and-white, sober picture of Jesus in his **Gospel According to Matthew.** It is true that his non-smiling young Jesus strides through the film with great vigour and intensity. A rugged Jesus seems to be preferable to a sweet Jesus. However, Pasolini has used the same method for making his 'realistic' Jesus: the 20th century literal reading of the New Testament. While Pasolini's reading is stark, a Jesus confronting authority and making serious demands on his followers (Jesus-Marxist?), it is not entirely the Jesus of the real Gospel according to Matthew.

It was only in the '70s with **Jesus of Nazareth,** made for television but released world-wide first in cinemas, the creative collaboration of Franco Zeffirelli and his screenwriter Anthony Burgess (author of **A Clockwork Orange**), that a more researched Jesus was presented.

Zeffirelli has a great deal of Old Testament background in his film. Jewish and Roman history is also included via characters and pointed speeches. There is a very strong sense of the Gospels as the preached good news about Jesus, as preached portraits of Jesus rather than biographies or histories of his life. Zeffirelli rearranges Gospel incidents (as did the Gospel-writers themselves) to highlight his themes.

An excellent example is the presentation of the popular parable of the prodigal son. Zeffirelli has Jesus speak this parable at a banquet of tax-collectors and sinners as St. Luke's Gospel suggests. However, he makes the banquet much more explicit in that it is a banquet hosted by his new disciple Matthew. The point of the parable is made even stronger, not just by the criticisms of the scribes and pharisees, as Luke's Gospel suggests, but by the criticism of his main disciple, Peter himself. Peter has refused to go in to

Matthew's banquet. He remains outside. There is talk about how much forgiveness should be offered to those who ask it — seventy times seven?

The parable is then directed, not only to the critical scribes and pharisees but also to Peter the critical disciple, the equivalent of the older son. Peter overhears the parable from outside and is moved and changed by it.

Visually Zeffirelli has not relied solely on 19th century popular art styles, but has used the wider tradition of Christian art. His realistic 'Jesus-figure' is more authentic and more accessible. ■

GODSPELL . . . *The conventions of vaudeville, the musical, the carnival are used to interpret the Gospel story.*

9

Stylised Jesus-figures

*While most attempts
to present Jesus on the screen
have used the realistic style,
more recent portrayals have returned
to an old artistic tradition:
stylising the presentations of Jesus,
situating him in
more contemporary settings and styles.*

The story and the person of Jesus have excited the western imagination (Christian and non-Christian alike) through the centuries and the challenge of presenting him to contemporary audiences has always appealed. Jesus walks in lovely Umbrian countrysides in Mediaeval and Renaissance frescoes. Jesus looks particularly Dutch in the sombre shadows and glows of Rembrandt. Brueghel and Bosch could situate Jesus somewhere in a Germanic hell on earth. It has been respectable to present Jesus-figures in the artistic framework of the times. The same is true of music, and Bach has dignified the Passion with his sacred score.

While this could be theoretically accepted, around 1970 new hymns or contemporary music were acceptable ways of presenting Jesus-figures. The words 'rock', 'superstar', 'opera' were then to be associated with him and prevail.

The record of **Jesus Christ, Superstar** was argued about in the early '70s — the contemporary musical idiom provided not only difficulties, it provided a barrier, and many of the public were offended. Yet Tim Rice and Andrew Lloyd Webber, in imaginative lyrics and contemporary sounds, were presenting a Jesus-figure — not rewriting the Gospels or diminishing them as was the accusation. The stage version had razzamatazz and show-biz extravaganza. The techniques were to induce the atmosphere of the rock opera to focus on the experience of **Jesus Christ, Superstar.**

Norman Jewison's film version had echoes of the stage presentation but sought ways of bringing the rock opera to the widest audience possible. There was a greater air of reverence (rightly or wrongly) for Christian sensibilities in the film. It was interesting to note that Ted Nealy, who portrayed Jesus in the modern troupe's enactment of the music in Israel and in the Judaean desert, did not get back into the bus at the end of the film; a silhouette of a shepherd was seen on a distant hill in the setting sun — symbols of resurrection perhaps? There had been criticisms that the Resurrection was omitted from the stage version.

Jesus Christ, Superstar was an explicitly 20th century re-enactment of the Gospels — a play within a play so to speak — but it legitimised the characterisation, the liberties taken with the Gospel text, and the modern tone, especially Jesus' anguish. A similar thing was done by playwright Denis Potter in his B.B.C. television play, **The Son of Man.** Again, audiences at the time found it difficult to take the presentation of Jesus in agony in Gethsemane, questioning whether this suffering was happening to him. A fundamentalist reading of Scripture was unable to absorb the meaning of a stylised Jesus-figure.

Godspell was described as a sweet rock opera. Again there was re-enactment, this time in New York locations. The conventions of the musical, burlesque, and old movies were incorporated to bring the good news and the sayings, parables and actions of Jesus to life. The atmosphere of clowns and clowning enhanced the humour and the pathos of **Godspell.** Both **Jesus Christ, Superstar** and **Godspell** were contemporary interpretations of Jesus — they presupposed a more interpretative reading of the Gospels than the biblical epics did. They took a greater liberty and gave greater freedom in presenting Jesus-figures on the screen.

Two examples of Jesus-figures from the early '70s illustrate the kind of freedom reached. The Jesus-figures offer insight — but they do so by comparisons and by shock or surprise.

In the middle of Dalton Trumbo's **Johnny Got His Gun,** we have the hero, a limbless head and torso, almost desensitised by injuries in World War I, in a military hospital. However, his memory is alive, also his imagination. One night he dreams that Jesus is with him, working, talking in modern idiom, advising but also jolting his expectations about himself and his values. The actor was Donald Sutherland, dressed in the pious holy card style, but sounding quite different; there is a final image of him driving a steam engine and waving farewell through the hero's dream.

Another example is from a film by flamboyant director Ken Russell, who has depicted many Christ-figures and offers some shocking Jesus-figures. In **The Devils,** he visually explored religious hysteria in the France of the religious wars of the 17th century. The superior of the convent at Loudun is a hunchback of authoritarian manner and repressed sexuality. She is portrayed by Vanessa Redgrave. She has a passion for a local Jesuit priest, played by Oliver Reed. Ultimately she causes his death — torture and martyrdom — by which the audience sees him as another Christ. However, as she prays, she has blasphemous-looking fantasies where she sees Reed as Jesus walking on the water to her, as Jesus on the cross, where she is Mary Magdalene and he comes down to embrace her passionately.

Some audiences found these images alarming. However, they were visual attempts to dramatise this kind of mad religion.

Satirists have also used the stylised Jesus-figure for comment on contemporary society. Exiled Spanish director Luis Bunuel waged satirical cinema war on Spanish Catholicism. In **The Milky Way,** his characters on pilgrimage to Compostella enter into Gospel episodes: the carpenter's shop at

Nazareth with Jesus about to shave and a statue-like Mary persuading him to keep his beard, Jesus at Cana and questions about his ability to laugh. Bunuel is asking questions about traditional theological issues by satiric dramatisation. This is not, of course, to everyone's taste and it provokes controversy.

Mel Brooks, a writer of very broad comedy, inserts a Last Supper sequence into his **History of the World Part One** with some verbal jokes about the current use of Jesus' name as an expletive, plus parody of Leonardo da Vinci's painting.

Stylised Jesus-figures are acceptable when reverent, controversial when offbeat or irreverent.

Just when film-makers told audiences that there was no future in Biblical epics, bitter controversy broke out world-wide in August 1988. The focus of argument was the (generally unseen) version by director Martin Scorsese and writer Paul Schrader of **The Last Temptation of Christ** by Greek thinker and novelist, Nikos Kazantzakis.

The look of the film is gritty and realistic, reinforcing the offensiveness for audiences who took the film literally. But Kazantzakis (and Scorsese) state this is a stylised, very personal interpretation of Jesus. Written in earthy Greek, the novel becomes an '80s New York-accented movie.

Visual stylising abounds: Scorsese's blood motif at crucifixions, with Jesus' Sacred Heart, Peter eating the Last Supper bread, blood dripping from his mouth; the temptation emblems, especially Jesus' guardian angel, in reality Satan. Most striking is the Crucifixion hallucination where, Jesus, about to die, agonising about his mission, imagines being permitted to descend from the cross to lead a quietly ordinary family life, grow old and die. This is Kazantzakis' 'last temptation': to ordinariness instead of saviour-heroism.

Long, evocative, provocative, not a Gospel portrait of Jesus, Scorsese's personal film is a singular interpretation of the Gospel story meant for 20th-century questioners and searchers, be they believers or non-believers. ∎

AGNES OF GOD . . . *Meg Tilly plays Agnes, the 'Agnus Dei', the Lamb of God, the innocent sacrificial victim.*

10

Jesus as Redeemer

*One of the principal ways
the New Testament presents Jesus
is as a Redeemer,
the man amongst mankind
who experiences their sufferings
but who suffers on behalf of others,
enabling them to be
blessed, forgiven — to be saved.*

The pattern of the redeemer-figure is established in the Old Testament. The key texts are those of the anonymous prophet of the period of Israel's collapse and exile in the 6th century B.C.

The Hebrew people had experienced the worst events in their history, a time of infidelity to their God who had, they understood, pledged himself to them in a covenant of loving kindness and justice. The disaster of the destruction of Jerusalem, of the temple and the loss of the Ark of the Covenant, the structure containing the Ten Commandments (their covenant law) — all was seen as The Day of the Lord, a day of doom (justice) but, because of the fidelity of God, a day of hope (salvation). The majority of the population of the kingdom of Judah was taken into exile in Babylon.

This context of bitter experience is a context of suffering in which the redeemer-figure can emerge.

The anonymous prophet in the second part of Isaiah seems to be a literary hero, a personality who embodies the best qualities of Israel, and is depicted as a prophet and redeemer. He is presented in the traditional Servant Songs which begin at chapter 42 of the Book of Isaiah. This figure is a character with a special mission and destiny. He is beloved by God, chosen, filled with the very spirit of God himself. His style is not that of power but of gentleness. If a flame is still smouldering, he will not extinguish it. If a reed is bruised, he will not break it. But this gentleness has strength and will enable true justice to be done, not only for his people but far beyond. He is described as a Light of the Nations. (Isaiah 42:1-4)

This kind of figure, no matter how admirable, does not win acclaim from all. When people are challenged, when different values threaten an accepted way of life, reaction is hostile. So it was with the anonymous figure who is now called 'The Servant'. He is attacked emotionally and physically. But, with his sense of mission, he listens like a disciple to his God, and with his convictions, he holds firm. This leads to mockery, abuse, degradation and death.

The image offered is that of the sacrificial lamb. However, the writer realises that, while those who see this 'man of sorrows' are appalled, his willingness to endure the suffering is a jolt to those who watch. The Servant going to suffering and death is 'a man for others'.

The jolt, the challenge can be what we might call an experience of grace for others, a change of heart (a repentance) that enables them to redeem the evil in their lives. The Servant is, therefore, a redeemer. While the Old Testament texts speak of his being acknowledged (glorified) by God, the emphasis is on his suffering and death: laying down of life for love and for the benefit of others. (Cf. Isaiah 52:12-53:12)

Readers of the Old Testament appreciated the Servant-figure in connection with other suffering figures. Just prior to the exile, the most human of the prophets, Jeremiah, exercised a faithful ministry — but at great personal cost. Even the story of his prophetic call shows him as quite reluctant. He was not listened to. Crowds scorned him. The king literally cut up and burnt the scrolls of his oracle. He was thrown into a pit. Yet ultimately he 'committed' his cause to God.

There are powerful passages, called his Confessions, in which he berates God, threatens to sue him, take him to court; he laments the day he was born. Unlike the men of his day who found immortality in their children, he was asked to be celibate. Yet he confesses that there is a fire in him that drives him on to be a prophetic redeemer. (Cf. Jeremiah 15:15-18)

Prayers of suffering are found throughout the Psalms.

The other Old Testament figure of anguish and endurance is that of Job. He is written of as God's victim. God allows one member of his heavenly court (according to the Old Testament mentality), the Satan (the Devil's Advocate), to test, to plague Job. It is well known that Job did not curse God in any way; he suffered — not silently, because he wanted to know why he suffered, because he knew he was in no way a sinner despite the carping of his friends (or comforters!).

Job is the symbol of all those innocent victims, the endurers who have to acknowledge the mystery of human existence and throw themselves on the mystery of God's ultimate providence and love. (Cf. Job 3:1-26; 19:23-27)

These are the patterns for the New Testament presentation of Jesus. He is seen to be Redeemer. While, like the Servant, he is beloved by God, he is baptised by John the Baptist among the repentant sinners in the Jordan. The Letter to the Hebrews highlights that he is 'a man like us, with the exception of sin', and that, though ultimately he is raised and glorified by the Father, he knows human sufferings since he has endured them.

In Gethsemane, Jesus is ignored by sleeping friends, sweats blood, experiences agony and sudden fear and is prepared to endure, like the Servant, the scorn of religious authorities who have continually tried to trap him. He knows the fickleness of the loyalty of friends and followers, the physical abuse and torture of his passion, the seeming absence of and abandonment by God on his cross. He is the timeless image of the man of sorrows, the sacrificial lamb for others.

In the first letter of Peter, the author states directly that he sees Jesus as the redeemer-figure and quotes the Servant Songs of the Old Testament for his proof.

The pattern of Jesus as the man of sorrows, the man who died for humankind while forgiving his killers, has become part of the consciousness of western culture. Believers and unbelievers alike have been able to draw on the experience of Jesus as a metaphor or as a symbol of the suffering which does not turn in on itself in despair or bitterness but is offered to others for support, courage or endurance. The instrument of Jesus' death, the cross, has become the sign of this suffering for others.

This image of Jesus-redeemer has become in the arts the reference point for stories of innocent sufferers, so that they can be understood as Christ-figures, redeemer-figures. ■

THE OMEGA MAN . . . *After trying to save survivors of a nuclear catastrophe, Charlton Heston, the Omega Man, dies in a fountain, his heart pierced.*

11

Redeemer Figures in Film

*The redeemer-figure
bears a significant resemblance
to Jesus —
in relation to the human condition,
evil and sin and suffering
and death for others.*

Old and New Testaments highlight significant features of Jesus as redeemer. It is these features that are characteristic of the redeemer-figure. Not everyone who is portrayed as suffering and/or dying in a film can be interpreted as a cinema redeemer-figure. The resemblance needs to be important and substantial. The sufferer is, in a significant way, at the service of, at least, a fellow human being. The suffering is something of the equivalent of the Passion of Jesus and his crucifixion. This can be suggested verbally or, with the wide range of styles in iconography, visually.

Older moralising films tended to use an explicit Scripture text — of which one of the favourites was 'What doth it profit a man to gain the whole world and lose his soul?' (which was even used to introduce Bob Guccione's Penthouse **Caligula!**).

The redeemer-figure is caught up in the world of evil, of human sinfulness. This figure is a victim of sin and its consequences. The redeemer-figure, by suffering, also condemns this evil and sinfulness and is able to atone for it or reconcile sinners. The character may be redeemed by his or her own suffering. They are also able to be the means of redemption for others.

Innocent suffering is the most obvious role for redeemer-figures. There are victims who suffer illness, disability, imprisonment, death for what seems to be no other reason than human or divine malice. These men and women suffer like Job. The Scriptures and history have many stories of children massacred, whether by Pharaoh in Egypt when Moses was saved, or in Bethlehem when Jesus was saved, or in the many wars, European ghettos, Vietnamese villages or among the starving in India or Africa.

Sometimes the innocent sufferer is presented symbolically as the human angel who is victimised precisely because of goodness, as in the case of Terence Stamp's portrayal of **Billy Budd.**

Vicarious suffering — the laying down of life for others — is the most often portrayed. It is a frequent feature of westerns. Along with buddy-heroism, it is also a feature of many war films. One remembers the action of Oates in the Antarctic expedition, dramatised in **Scott of the Antarctic,** where he knew he was dying and walked out into the snow so that the rest of the expedition could have more food and a better chance to get back to base and safety.

Jesus stressed that this was true human heroism — the greatest love that one human being could give to another. He also said that if his disciples did this, it would be the most impressive way that they could show themselves to be his disciples.

Christian martyrs like Becket or universal martyrs like Gandhi are significant examples of this kind of witnessing to convictions in courage.

But most redeemer-figures are not only caught up in the sinful world, they are often a significant part of it. One might note that the only sinless redeemer-figures are Jesus himself and his mother Mary. Paul is quick to point out that while he urges his fellow Christians to be imitators of him as he is of Christ, he is by no means perfect himself.

In a famous passage (Rom.7:15-20,) he says, 'I cannot understand my own behaviour. I fail to carry out the things I want to do and I find myself doing the very things I hate ... For though the will to do what is good is in me, the performance is not, with the result that instead of doing the good things I want to do, I carry out the sinful things I do not want'.

This means that the Jobs, the Innocents, the Billy Budds are the exceptional redeemer-figures. It means that in the complexities of the drama, the redeemer-figure can be both evil and good.

In **High Plains Drifter,** Clint Eastwood portrays a mysterious figure who rides into a western town, saves the poor and the victims, then, literally, paints the town red, putting a sign at the entrance, 'Hell'. He sets the town alight in the night and stands in the flames cracking a whip, punishing the villains. In a sense he is a Christ-figure and a Devil-figure at the same time. And Paul asks in the letter to the Romans whether this is not true of us all.

Charles Dickens in his **Tale of Two Cities** character, Sidney Carton, shows us a man who is weak, a shambles character, drinking and cynical but who has the inner resources to voluntarily take the place of a man condemned to the guillotine and utter the well-known redeemer-figure words, 'It is a far, far better thing I do ...'

At one stage of his career, Paul Newman seemed to be specialising in this kind of character. He was able to portray the battler as well as the hustler.

In **Cool Hand Luke** he combined both: he was the good-humoured drifter, capable of better things but who exerted most of his energy in challenging authority and escaping from prison. Likable, he unwittingly gathered followers who put their faith in him. Cornered in his escape, he is pursued into an empty church where he prays, not the certain prayer of former centuries when a man knew that God was listening and had faith that his prayer would be heard; Luke prays as a man looking at himself and others, wondering what it is all about; he calls out to the 'old man up there' to come and say something to him. It is an image of much modern prayer — a shout of inquiry whether God up there can hear.

God doesn't say anything. Luke really didn't expect he would. That's how life is — and cool, smiling Luke, who doesn't have much to live for here, is ready to die. He is shot to death.

The redeemer-figure style was even more evident (in retrospect we see it as part of the interest in anti-heroes and disillusionment in the mid-and late '60s) in another western, **Hombre.** The title is a version of Man, Son of Man, or, better, Everyman. Newman portrays John Russell, part-Indian, part-white, a victim in the 19th century American west. In the west's version of the microcosm, the stagecoach, Russell travels with a motley collection of good people and some ruthless sinners. The group is besieged and desperately needs water. The only person who can help is John Russell. There is no reason for him to help. In fact, he has vengeful grounds for leaving some of them to die. He does not. In his attempt to save their lives, he loses his.

Hombre is fairly explicit in presenting its central character powerfully via the screen presence of Paul Newman, as a selfless redeemer.

In times of doubt and disillusionment, the redeemer-figure offers some notion of meaning, reconciliation and atonement. ∎

ABSENCE OF MALICE . . . *Sally Field as an ambitious journalist who targets a wealthy businessman, Paul Newman, almost destroying his reputation unjustly.*

12

Martyr Figures: Witnesses

*The dying Jesus
can be seen as a martyr,
witnessing publicly
to his convictions and commitment.
Martyrs, executed or assassinated,
have been a feature of history
and remain so today.*

The redeemer-figure is one who expects suffering, even death. The greatest selfless suffering is vicarious suffering. Some of those who die give a testimony by their death to the meaning of their lives and their personal integrity. It is these sufferers we call martyrs.

The title 'martyr' comes from the Greek word for 'witness'. The martyr is a witness to the world, whether this is deliberately intended or not, and to those who persecute, that a cause or a principle or a commitment is utterly and ultimately important. The martyr makes strong convictions visible, and death is the final witness. It is there for all to see that commitment is a matter of life and death.

In the early Christian era, the martyrs worried officials in the Roman Empire who saw them as subverting the authority of the emperor and the state. Missionaries, from the Dark Ages to the opening up of the New World, to 19th century evangelists in Africa or Oceania, have met opposition and death. Political dictatorships of both Left and Right have imprisoned, tortured and killed in our time. The films of Costa Gavras, **Z, The Confession, Missing** dramatise these contemporary persecutions and atrocities.

In an age of terrifyingly spectacular arms developments and build-ups, the martyr is no longer necessarily tried and executed. Assassination is the brutal method. Docu-dramas of 20th century celebrities (one thinks of Martin Luther King) remind us of this martyrdom continually. The anti-nuclear protestors are saying, at least, that they do not wish the world to be assassinated. We do not want apocalypse now.

The Christian way of telling martyrs' stories derives from the end of the Old Testament era, from the time of the invasion of Palestine by Syria, the consequent religious persecution and the guerrilla resistance by the Maccabees and their followers. The second book of Maccabees 6-7 tells the story of the old man Eleazar who refused to offer incense to the gods and wanted to avoid giving scandal, and of the seven sons and their mother who gave outspoken witness speeches defying King Antiochus.

These stories became the models for similar Jewish stories and early Christian accounts of persecution, The Acts of the Martyrs, and shaped the reverent (though not afraid of some blood and guts detail) style of reporting the martyrs' heroic deaths. The biblical and early Christian costume screen spectaculars took their tone from them.

Jesus is also presented as a martyr. He incurred the animosity of many of the religious leaders who, proud of their commitment to the tradition of their fathers, reacted angrily to Jesus' activity, either condemning him as too easy in his interpretation (and breaking) of the Law or attacking him as being disloyal to civil authorities.

The Gospels present Jesus as speaking with authority and in the language of the Old Testament. He attacked the religious leaders for their rigidity and double standards. Always trying to catch and trap him, they arrested and tried him, eventually defying him to state his own convictions, which he did before the High Priest Caiaphas and the Roman governor Pilate. He was executed, martyred between two thieves, the type of person that he attracted to repentance, much to the disgust of his enemies.

The Acts of the Martyrs style was seen in the earliest Australian religious screen production, **Soldiers of the Cross** (1899), a Salvation Army evening of lecture, slides and film. Dramatic scenes from the early church exalting the martyrs were played against backdrops draped on tennis court fences. Cecil B. De Mille's **Sign of the Cross** (1932) gave us almost instant conversions and the Christians thrown to the lions. Colourful '50s spectacles like **Quo Vadis, The Robe, Demetrius and the Gladiators, The Silver Chalice** and **The Big Fisherman** all reinforced these images for the large cinema-going public.

More credible films of martyrdom included **Becket,** with Richard Burton playing the outspoken Archbishop of Canterbury. (There had also been a little-seen small-budget film of T. S. Eliot's **Murder in the Cathedral** in the '50s). This kind of Church-State confrontation was dramatised during the period of communist trials of Catholics in eastern Europe in the '50s. The best of these was **The Prisoner** with Alec Guinness.

Documentary dramas and telemovies have become popular in bringing contemporary political stories to the screen very quickly. The Kennedys have been popular subjects of such films.

From Poland has come the less direct presentation of contemporary issues — for instance in the work of Andrej Wajda, especially his **Man of Marble** and **Man of Iron,** focusing on industrial relations and Solidarity, as well as his **Danton** which parallels the confrontation between Robespierre and Danton (with Danton's execution) and General Jaruselski and Lech Walesa in the early '80s.

In a different political context, that of Indonesia in 1965, the Chinese-Australian dwarf Billy Kwan at the centre of **The Year of Living Dangerously** is a significant martyr-figure. Ridiculed by fellow journalists with such jibes as 'get down from the cross', Billy quotes Luke 3:10, 'What then must we do?', the reply to John the Baptist of those who were converted. Billy decides that he can help only those he knows, aiding a poor family, guiding his friends. He trusts in President Soekarno. But when the child he tends dies, he becomes disillusioned with Soekarno and makes a dramatic witness gesture, hanging a condemning banner from a hotel Soekarno is to pass (but he never sees it), and allows himself to be shot by the military. The Christ-figure martyr language is explicit.

In recent decades attitudes to martyr-figures have changed, a greater allowance being made for sin in a martyr's life. In **The Fugitive,** the '40s version of Graham Greene's **The Power and the Glory,** Henry Fonda's priest is much more edifying than the central character in the novel. In fact, he is not a whisky-priest, nor does he live with the woman. Instead he is portrayed as a man afraid, willing to escape danger and too proud. Greene's point of heroism in priestly ministry — the priest knowing he was being betrayed for money by a character referred to as Judas — still remains. The point of martyrdom is clear but the priest is yet another of Henry Fonda's upright screen characters.

The '60s version, **The Power and the Glory,** with Laurence Olivier, remains closer to the novel and has the ambivalent drama of the sinner-priest who, though weak, is graced to be a priest-martyr.

The martyr-figure is usually someone in the public eye, an edifying person. More and more today, the witness of martyrdom is a reality for any human being. ■

HUNCHBACK OF NOTRE DAME . . . *While the Elephant Man was the nineteenth century suffering man of gentle dignity, his fictional equivalent was Hugo's hunchback (Anthony Hopkins).*

Job Figures:
Innocent Sufferers

The experience of innocent sufferers
has been an ages-long mystery.
Some see it as the 'problem of evil',
others as the 'mystery of suffering'.
Like Job, there are many
innocent suffering-figures.

While we know that part of the human condition is to suffer, we are prepared to accept suffering in the context of justice, atonement and reconciliation. We also accept the generosity and self-giving of suffering so that those we love will not have to suffer. But one of the greatest mysteries is what is termed 'the problem of evil', evil and suffering for innocent victims. Often the frustration and anger at this 'unjust suffering' is directed against God, who, though said to be all-loving, is blamed for the pain and anguish.

There are theological answers that have validity but are little help in comforting or soothing the sufferer: God, who is love, gives us our freedom; evil is human, disasters are part of nature and not directly willed by God; suffering in this world is brought about by human sinfulness.

God's own answer is Jesus himself. Becoming part of this world's experience, he suffered physical, mental and spiritual anguish, dying a disgraceful death. Jesus cannot take away the suffering but he can offer the painful experience of his own in sympathy and empathy. Ultimately, he offers new life and resurrection.

Two phrases have been used: 'problem of evil' and 'mystery of suffering'. It is worth noting that the first is more of a speculative question. Problems, no matter how difficult, are to be solved. And the insights of philosophy and theology can go a long way to solving the problem to some enquirers' satisfaction.

The second phrase is much more personal, experiential. Real people really suffer. And suffering is not a problem to be solved. Mysteries, unlike problems, cannot be solved. One can enter more and more into a mystery: understand, feel, live it. This is, of course, what Jesus himself has done and why his suffering experience is not meant to be a problem-solving device but is a sharing deeply in the mystery.

It is in the light of this presentation of Jesus, that we can consider the next group of redeemer-figures: Job-figures. Not only has Job become the biblical representative of the innocent sufferer, he has become part of world literature.

In the 6th and 5th centuries B.C., the Jews tried to grapple with the mystery of suffering and their gracious covenant God. They did not have the (comparatively) easy way out of the mystery in an after-life, a heaven. At this stage of their history, unlike, for instance, their Egyptian neighbours, they had no real conception of a life after death. Everything was experienced here on earth.

Job, a wealthy patriarch (whose clan reminds us of that of Abraham) is struck, deprived, tormented by the Satan, the 'Devil's advocate'. Despite pain and anguish, criticisms from wife and alleged comforter-friends, he does not curse God. He proclaims his innocence, he proclaims that God is good. The mystery is too much for him to grasp. Job is the exemplary sufferer, a pattern for those of us who cannot stay with his faith. The prophet Jeremiah, whom Job sometimes resembles, finally declares, 'I commit my cause to God'. If he is good, as he is, there must be and will be some meaning. (Jeremiah 20:12)

In our time, as in so many centuries, the Jews have suffered like Job. The experience of the Holocaust — and a holocaust is a sacrifice where the victim is utterly destroyed — has become a 20th century symbol of the victim-sufferer. From television mini-series to feature films, **Holocaust, The Diary of Anne Frank, Playing for Time, The Hiding Place,** our screens abound with these figures touching heart and conscience.

The handicapped and the disabled, the blind, deaf, lame are all Job-redeemer-figures. The screen has not been short of factual and fictional stories of painful lives redeemed, new lives. The popularity of these stories, which are sometimes characterised by special pleading and even sentimentality, indicates the need for a more subtle appreciation of the lives of such people.

Heroes (**Reach for the Sky**), sports-figures (**Joni, The Other Side of the Mountain**), singers (**Interrupted Melody**) as well as characters like Jane Wyman's deaf-mute in **Johnny Belinda** are examples.

One of the most moving screen-characters portraying extreme disability is John Hurt as **The Elephant Man.** The screenplay opted for making audiences appreciate John Merrick, the elephant man, as a person by not showing him and his disfigurement for about thirty minutes. Audiences saw only others' reactions. Tension was created as audiences waited to look at Merrick and then, unexpectedly, he was seen. But he was seen as a human being. Physically deformed and treated by the ugly underside of prim Victorian society as a side-show freak, he nevertheless was a man of great dignity, which was revealed in sequences of his reciting the 23rd Psalm and playing a Romeo and Juliet scene. Tormented at a railway station, he calls out desperately but truly, 'I am a man'. **The Elephant Man** is one of the most moving of such suffering figures.

The Depression was a period that offered many stories of suffering not only for individuals but for families and large groups of men and women wandering and searching for work. One of the most striking films about the Depression was the version of Steinbeck's **The Grapes of Wrath.** Henry Fonda, as Tom Joad, stood for the ordinary American victim of nature, society and fellow human beings hoping against hope for a future.

On the level of the very ordinary man, Hitchcock's **The Wrong Man** is an experience of a man mistakenly arrested for hold-ups in New York, charged and tried. Hitchcock himself had a dread from childhood of being locked up in a police station. This is frighteningly communicated as audiences could identify the real possibilities of such events happening to them. Henry Fonda portrayed the wrong man. Police station, prison and courtroom sequences had a heightened eeriness as the wrong man was trapped and enmeshed in a tightening tangle of circumstantial evidence. The impact was compounded by the suffering of his wife, played by Vera Miles, who gradually collapsed emotionally and mentally, associated her husband's misfortunes with her imagined shortcomings as a wife.

The Wrong Man is an effectively distressing film about innocent suffering.

In a society where a religious faith seems to be lived by a minority, theological answers on evil and suffering are not always persuasive. The experience of Jesus has been a source of consolation. Others rely heroically on a stoic acceptance of suffering. The Job-figures, however, give a pattern for faith in anguish. ■

DUNE . . . *Paul Atreides (Kyle Machlan), the warrior-saviour foretold in Frank Herbert's saga.*

14

Jesus as Saviour

In the New Testament Jesus is called Lord.
After his living as a human being,
like us — sin excepted —
he was raised from the dead,
the Risen Saviour who leads the way
to joy, peace — the salvation of 'Heaven'.

The first striking Old Testament story concerns Abraham, the head of a large clan on the now Persian Gulf who, like many clans of the time (about 1800 B.C.), took part in nomadic migrations. Abraham's clan eventually settled in the land of Canaan, later Palestine, which became for them home, a promised land, rich and fruitful, flowing with milk and honey. Though much of it was arid mountain and desert, it was, nevertheless, their paradise homeland.

However, the reason for Abraham's migration was his experience of his God. He felt a sense of call, of destiny for himself, his descendants, not just the establishing of a dynasty, but a people responsible to their God and devoted to him, a 'chosen' people. We remember that the early centuries of their history were marked by squabbles and bitterness, but also by joy and reconciliation.

After many of them stayed in Egypt for hundreds of years, they were oppressed by the Pharaoh, made slaves and, in a mass escape, led by Moses, went out of Egypt into the desert forming themselves into a people, exhilarated by liberation, on their way back home to the land of Abraham, a promised land that they saw as their inheritance.

Old Testament writers, listening to the stories remembered and repeated from these times and passed on orally for generations, realised that there was a deep religious meaning in these events. Their God had acted for them in their history. They were oppressed and needed liberating. He freed them, he saved them. They were a sinful people. He freed them from their sinfulness, he forgave them. They were a chosen people and their God had pledged himself to them — to be just, loving, faithful no matter how unfaithful his people were.

This union of God and his people, this Covenant (with its laws, especially the Ten Commandments) became the sign of salvation. Old Testament personages were remembered and written of in connection with this Covenant: leaders like Moses and Joshua, the judge Samuel, Kings Saul, David, Solomon.

Needless to say, chosen people do not remain faithful. They turn away from their fidelity in personal sin, social sin, especially injustice. They need forgiveness and salvation. In the Old Testament history of Israel, the main figures who embodied this message of salvation were the prophets, a group who, intermittently, for over 200 years showed by their words, their oracles, their symbolic actions and by their own lives that God was a saving God.

In looking at the religious experience and the messages of such diverse personalities as the rugged shepherd Amos, the tender Hosea, the statesman Isaiah, the reluctant and persecuted Jeremiah, the exotic Ezekiel, we see God's fidelity to his people in offering his salvation.

It was little wonder that New Testament writers drew on Covenant themes but, especially, the experiences and words of the prophets when they wanted to show that Jesus was a saviour. It is the constant theme of the Gospels that Jesus was this kind of figure: a prophetic saviour.

A phrase that the Old Testament prophets used was The Day of the Lord. For a while, the Hebrew people were presumptuous enough to think that this meant that God would sweep away all their enemies and they would live in power, prosperity and peace. (Many zealots of Jesus' day still had the same hope and followed Jesus because of it but were disappointed when he was found not to be the restorer of the kingdom of Israel.)

What the prophets really meant by The Day of the Lord was a day both of justice and salvation. There would be justice because the evil in the hearts and actions of the people would inevitably bring down on themselves some decay, moral weakness and destruction. This was interpreted as the hand of the Lord striking them.

But The Day of the Lord was also the time for re-assessment, a change of heart — repentance — a humble and more realistic attitude so that whatever the disaster and destruction, a renewed fidelity could carry the people through. They might only be few: a remnant. But they could be the foundation of a renewed growth. Prophets like Jeremiah and Ezekiel said that for people like this, God would take out their hard hearts (like stone) and put in hearts of flesh, a 'fresh-hearted' remnant, people with 'new heart'. It would be a second Covenant. We recognise this as the language of Jesus and of the New Testament.

The Hebrew people were not a nation of scholarly philosophers. Rather, they were imaginative, poetic, a people of experience, especially religious experience. The way they expressed themselves was in concrete rather than abstract language: new hearts, shepherds leaving sheep to graze and rest, dry bones in a valley coming to life with flesh and becoming human again, fruitful vines, banquets of the best food and drink when those who are faithful are forgiven, healed and gathered together to rejoice.

These images were developed over the centuries by many writers. For instance, David was a shepherd before becoming king; kings are seen as shepherds, bad kings being bad shepherds, good kings being good shepherds; the great king and, therefore, the good (best) shepherd is God himself, who listens to his sheep, guides them and rescues them when they are lost. Jesus and the New Testament writers use these images for signs and symbols of salvation. They quickly became constant themes for Christian art, poetry, hymns. They still are. So many of Jesus' own stories rely on this kind of imagery for their impact and meaning.

Even the Servant-figure of the Old Testament who willingly gave his painful suffering and his death for the sake of others, is spoken of, finally, in words of joy and exultation. Every redeemer-figure is, ultimately, a saviour. That is why Jesus' passion and death can be described so vividly in Old Testament language. But it is not a despairing description; there is hope.

The Christian meaning is death — and resurrection. J. R. Tolkien, author of **The Lord of the Rings,** created a fine word to describe this: eucatastrophe. The Greek word for 'well' is **eu.** So for Tolkien (and for the Gospel-writers), for those who believe in salvation from God, suffering, which is real and painful, is, nevertheless, a eucatastrophe. ■

THE OUTLAW JOSEY WALES . . . *Clint Eastwood starred in and directed one of the best saviour-figure Westerns.*

15

Saviour Figures: Liberators

Saviour-figures have a significant resemblance
to Jesus who died but was raised to a new life.
A graced leader, he brought salvation
to those in need.

While redeemer-figures resemble Jesus particularly in his suffering and death, the saviour-figures focus more on resurrection. A saviour-figure can and does suffer, but the meaning of the figure is more in leadership, in rescuing and saving, in helping fellow human beings to a destiny that images paradise. Words that come to mind in association with the saviour are freedom, liberation, joy, fulfilment, peace and rest.

Scholars analysing the notion of leadership have emphasised that in times of crisis, a significant personality can emerge and meet the needs, 'rising to the occasion'. Sociologists have named this kind of leader 'charismatic', a gifted person whose talents and abilities are what the situation requires. They did not mean it necessarily to have religious connotations. There are any number of warrior-heroes in epic poems who are charismatic leaders, from Samson slaying the Philistines to Resistance leaders and revolutionaries like Castro or Lech Walesa.

However, charism is a word that has New Testament connotations as well — the gift of grace from God which transforms persons and fills them with God's Spirit. St. Paul says that this one Spirit provides a variety of gifts for the building up of the body of Christ which is the church. 'There is a variety of gifts but always the same Spirit; there are all sorts of services to be done, but always to the same Lord; working in all sorts of different ways in different people, it is the same God who is working in all of them. The particular way in which the Spirit is given to each person is for a good purpose.' (1 Cor.12:4-7) This meaning of 'charismatic' gained currency in many denominations, including the Catholic Church, during the '70s with the prayer movement of what is called Charismatic Renewal.

The two meanings of charism, the secular meaning of outstanding leader and the religious meaning of graced leader, are both relevant to the meaning of the saviour-figure.

The crisis that the saviour meets can have two aspects. Some evil may have caused it. In fact, evil draws down disaster on itself; it can be destructive. There is a crying out for justice to be done. But the survivors of the crisis, sometimes only a few, a remnant, experience a salvation and a joy. In the Old Testament, this kind of crisis was a Day of the Lord, a day of justice and a day of salvation.

The Old Testament also gives us a word to describe a saviour-figure. At first, the kings, then later individuals who showed leadership qualities, were called 'the Anointed One', 'Messiah'. The word and its adjective, messianic, have come into the English language. But the biblical messiahs were individuals who were chosen by God, not self-proclaimed. They listened to God's Word, received his Spirit and exercised their leadership in a 'prophetic' way.

Nowadays some individuals take up causes, trying to pressurise followers and are ridiculed as self-proclaimed messiahs. One thinks of fanatic sect leaders like Jim Jones of Guyana. There is something diabolical about this kind of 'saviour'.

In American films, the western hero is potentially a saviour-figure. One of the most interesting, because well done and with the references fairly explicit, was Clint Eastwood's **The Outlaw Josey Wales.** As the film went on, one noticed that even the name Josey had a sound resembling Jesus.

The film opens with suffering and direct biblical references. In the pre-credits prologue, we learn that Josey's family has been killed and his property destroyed by Merrill's Marauders after the Civil War. As Josey buries the dead, the wooden cross he has placed on a grave leans on his shoulders and he repeats the words of Job, 'The Lord gives, the Lord takes away, blessed be the name of the Lord'.

While the film is a vengeance western, Josey is still a Christ-figure. After all, the Christ-figure is good but not perfect; there is also evil in the heart. As Josey pursues the killers, he undergoes a journey of change and of transformation. He also acquires followers: an old Indian chief, who no longer is able to get the 'edge' on people as stealthily stalking Indians should, and a retarded girl and her grandmother. These 'poor in spirit' characters become his faithful band, the camera often highlighting their procession behind Josey.

However, the film moves to allegory by the end. They search for and settle in a valley called Paradise. While they defend it against the Indians by shooting from the cruciform windows of a church, Josey and the Indian chief do not kill each other but rather exchange 'words of life'. The films that Clint Eastwood directs (as distinct from his starring vehicles directed by others) tend to have some symbolic hero connotations.

A major saviour-figure film and significant box-office success was **E.T.** Writer Melissa Mathison, commenting on critics' reaction to the children's fantasy and citing **The Wizard of Oz,** said she preferred the similarity to **Peter Pan.** She added 'And then there is the Christ-symbolism'. Although she apparently did not intend it at first, Mathison, who is Catholic school-educated, noticed the similarities, and that Jesus' story is a model for so many stories of meaning for life.

The resemblances are parallels rather than exact. The constant danger of analogies is that they can be taken too far and lose credibility. It is not impossible to say that Jesus is an E.T. who came to earth to do good and who still remains present, somehow, even though he has returned home. However, the point of Jesus coming to earth, quite unlike the friendly creature who was left behind lost and longs to call home, is that he became one like us sharing all our experiences with us.

The screenplay of **E.T.** does give some delightful and moving images of an extra-terrestrial living on earth: frightened, accepted, learning earth language and human communication, although with more knowledge and skills than the humans. Hunted by faceless authorities, he suffers, 'dies,' but by the mutual love for Eliot, he comes to a new life, rises, bequeaths his goodwill to his followers and ascends into the heavens.

Amid the delight, one can regret that more tears are shed over a lost E.T. than for so many starving children in our world and even over the story of the death of Jesus himself. But E.T. is a charming saviour-figure. Somebody remarked that after O.T. and N.T., E.T. might be interpreted as the Extra Testament!

As J. R. Tolkien reminded us, the saviour-figure suffers, undergoes a disaster, but the suffering finds meaning in some new life experience. And while this is a catastrophe, it is a 'eucatastrophe'. ■

KRULL . . . *Saviour-figures abound in the galaxies: Ken Marshall leads his men from the Canyon of the Firemares.*

16

Popular Saviours

Popular figures in an age
of instant and universal communication
are treated with awe but with slick style.
They become pop-figures.
The anti-hero gives way to the new hero,
the ordinary person who is given the opportunity
to fulfil dreams
or the new mythic characters —
be they here on earth or in space.

Luke Skywalker, Han Solo, Indiana Jones, Clark Kent (alias Superman) — along with his cousin Linda Lee (alias Supergirl) — might lay claim to being among the most widely-acknowledged saviour-figures of the '70s and '80s. They have the advantage of wide-screen presence and enormous promotional hype. But the fact is that they have not been ignored or dismissed as comic-strip extravaganza characters. They have commanded a following that cuts across international boundaries, cultures, ages and the sexes. All the world needs a saviour.

Until the mid-'70s, the heroic figures of films tended to be confused or alienated or even victims. Whether U.S. Bicentennial enthusiasm fostered it or not, from 1976 on we have the phenomenon of the pop-hero. The response to these pop-heroes indicates just how needed they were.

Sylvester Stallone wrote and starred in a boxing story of an ordinary, even mediocre, boxer from Philadelphia who was given the opportunity to come out of the ranks and fight a championship match. With Bill Conti's triumphant theme to back him, Stallone emerged as **Rocky** and the film went on to win the Oscar for Best Film of 1976. It gave millions of people a lift — the ordinary person can not only dream of being a hero but can be one. It requires effort, training, commitment. And victory, as well as suffering, can bring tears to the eyes.

There have been **Rocky** sequels and numerous spin-offs. The next year brought John Travolta's Tony Manero winning disco-dancing contests in **Saturday Night Fever** (and Stallone himself directed Travolta in the sequel **Staying Alive**). The music caught on, bright disco rhythms that took enthusiastic audiences through the achievements of **Fame,** the vigour of **Flashdance** and **Footloose** to **Breakdance** and **Beat Street** (almost a decade of heroism and success through dance).

But 1977 also brought the new heroes that delighted through three films, the **Star Wars** trilogy: Luke Skywalker, his sister Princess Leia and the sardonic Han Solo. The **Star Wars** films have become the myths of the '80s.

'The Gospel According to Peanuts' author Robert Short hit on the good news of these films and has written of 'The Gospel from Outer Space'. It is 'out there' in space and its galaxies, in ageless time (of ancient myths, mediaeval chivalry, Western codes and futuristic science-fantasy) that the perennial stories of good vs. evil, of the titanic struggles and battles, of the lowly hero called to be saviour-warrior (who must face and combat his shadow) are played out. And they are accessible to all.

In the direct plot-lines, in the one-dimensional characters and their comic-strip dialogue, they can be understood and appreciated by everyone. And they have been. They are the modern fairy-tales — George Lucas sees religion and fairy-tales interconnected, teaching us the right way to live and giving a moral anchor.

Whether screenwriters have intended it or not, the parallels to the Gospel stories are frequent. Luke Skywalker is the innocent young man with a mystery father, instructed by a wise warrior, Alec Guinness' Obi Ben Kenobi, who must, and does, save the galaxies from destruction, even to a final death-struggle with his father and a transformation to new life. Robert Short notes the link between Luke and George Lucas, the creator of **Star Wars** — even writing of the 'Gospel According to Lucas'!

Lucas' friend Steven Spielberg has his gospel from outer space brought to earth by **E.T.** But Spielberg has a tongue-in-cheek earthy variation of the heroic theme. Spielberg goes back to another source of pop-heroes, the Saturday matinee serial. Harrison Ford, so effective as Han Solo in **Star Wars,** plays his engagingly nonchalant hero, Indiana Jones, in a make-believe '30s setting with nothing more than his whip and his wits (but sometimes with a more than Plucky Heroine, or Cute Child — and a gun as a last resort). The religious touch is never far away with the Lost Ark of the Covenant or a Temple of Doom.

But the hero who came to earth to save the human race is **Superman.** Christopher Reeve combines charm, brawn and a sense of humour which sustained him through four **Superman** films. Under Richard Lester's direction the later films were entertainingly tricky spoofs and mythic hero extravaganzas at the same time. But writer Mario Puzo wrote a prologue to **Superman I** that made sense of its hero by parallels with Jesus.

On the planet of Krypton, in the Heavens, Jor-El (Marlon Brando moving from Godfather-figure to God the Father-figure) sends his only son to Earth. The vehicle looks a blend of crib and Magi star. On earth he grows up, hidden in Smallville U.S.A. with his foster parents until he receives his commission to go into his public life. As reporter Clark Kent, he covers his power. As Superman, the whole world is reassured that it has a saviour.

The danger with pop-heroes is derivative exploitation and rip-off. The cinema screens were awash with galactic adventures in the late '70s. Few of these films have stayed in memory. Rather, they enhanced the impact of the originals. Trends quickly come and go, but associated with the space chivalry came a round of mediaeval sword and sorcery films and excursions into the new world of video games where the universal battles were miniaturised as in **Tron** or paralleled the games, as in **The Last Starfighter.**

Meanwhile, back on earth, saviour-figures like **Billy Jack** fought for social and racial justice. Richard Dreyfus' Roy Neary led a group of suburban visionaries to Wyoming where friendly creatures from the other planets were to be closely encountered, in Steven Spielberg's **Close Encounters of the Third Kind. Tommy** led his rock opera disciples to climb the mountain to their fulfilment. ∎

EDUCATING RITA . . . *A vivacious Julie Walters, a contemporary 'wise clown', takes to learning with vigour and to Michael Caine with truth.*

17

Clown Figures:
Agents of Grace

While the word clown *might not seem*
immediately appropriate to Jesus,
his ironic humour in preaching and storytelling
and his being mocked in his passion
make him an admissible clown.
His imitators are recognisable Christ-figures.

A curiosity-rousing book was published in the '60s with the title, **The Humour of Jesus.** While it is remarked in the Gospels that Jesus wept, it is nowhere related that he laughed. Yet Jesus regretted that, while the scribes and the pharisees condemned John the Baptist as a madman because of his ascetic life-style, they accused him of being a wine-bibber and a glutton because he mixed with tax-collectors and prostitutes, especially at meals. At least, one might say that Jesus was not a gloomy man. Children, disciples, both men and women, the sick and the suffering all found him approachable.

Yet the humour of Jesus is a subtle, ironic twinkle of the eye and the nimble tongue. We sometimes do Jesus an injustice in reading the Gospels aloud with our churchy modulations and tones. For there are ironic touches, smiles and tongue-in-cheek in many parables: the details of the prodigal son and the sour older brother, the vain rhetoric of the pharisee against the publican, the man who built the huge barns and then immediately died.

Jesus could use images of splinters and beams in people's eyes, fathers possibly giving stones and scorpions to their children instead of bread or fish, and a pestering widow whose persistent and shameless nagging against an unjust judge is held up as a model for praying constantly without giving up hope. Most of these passages are in Luke's Gospel.

Jesus as preacher and storyteller had a way with words and was not above clowning.

On the grimmer side Jesus is treated as a clown in his Passion. He is slapped, ridiculed and dressed as a mock king with a reed sceptre and a crown of thorns. He is the servant from the book of Isaiah (chapter 53) — a man of sorrows who caused people to screen their faces, so disfigured did he seem. Jesus here is a sad clown, a butt of cruel jokes. As Pilate said, 'Behold the man'.

Clowns through history and literature have been funny and wise, happy and sad: jesters, buskers, mimes, fools, jokers, pranksters, sideshow oddities, circus performers.

Many comics of the screen have been clowns: Charlie Chaplin's tramp and little man, Buster Keaton's sad-faced hero, Harold Lloyd's ingenuous 'mishapper', Laurel and Hardy. Lon Chaney portrayed a clown in the '20s with the significant title **He Who Gets Slapped.** Clowns include Danny Kaye, Red Skelton, Jerry Lewis, Peter Sellers, Barbra Streisand and Woody Allen. Many of these stars have in fact portrayed clowns, especially circus clowns: Chaplin, **The Circus,** Skelton, **The Clown,** Lewis, **Three Ring Circus,** Sellers, **The Optimists.** Gene Kelly and Judy Garland sang 'Be a Clown' in **The Pirate;** Donald O'Connor was expert in 'Make 'Em Laugh' in **Singin' in the Rain.** The song from **A Little Night Music** was 'Send in the Clowns'.

Many explicitly religious films have taken up the theme of the Christ-figure clown. One of the best-known is the short film made for the 1964 New York World's Fair. It was called **Parable.** The figure could be interpreted as Jesus himself. Yet it seems more universal, more an 'Everyman' who embodies the best qualities of Jesus.

Prior to **Godspell,** this clown was rather unusual and striking. After **Godspell,** with its use of burlesque, carnival, movie routines, sets, styles and greasepaint, the clown is a more admissible Christ-figure.

Parable shows a circus representing the world, the powerful and the powerless: a water-carrier, an exploited beauty and a negro. Besides Magnus, the ring-master, there is a greedy ticket-seller, an angry animal-trainer, a tough customer who likes to pitch balls to dunk the negro.

The feature of the circus is a group of human puppets lifted high in the Big Top and manipulated, ultimately cruelly and berserkly, by Magnus. Enter behind the passing caravan parade the figure of a fool, a clown, completely white in skin and clothes, riding a donkey. Pursued by the greedy and exploitative, he is followed by the oppressed whose place he has taken or whom he has rescued. In the circus, watched by children, he takes the place of the human puppets, having them released. He is pulled disjointedly, racked to death. His followers mourn.

The parade goes by with its characteristic processional music. The figure in white is there again. He looked dead, he lives again and the parade goes on and by. In **Parable,** the central character is so obviously a Christ-figure that the detailed application of the incidents to Jesus indicates that it might be more accurately titled **Allegory.**

A fine film by Federico Fellini before he went in for more elaborate allegories of life with galleries of grotesque clowns, was his Oscar-winning **La Strada,** focusing on a cheap sideshow act with Anthony Quinn as Zampano the strong man. Richard Basehart plays Matto, literally 'the fool', who is killed by Zampano — a martyred goodness. Giulietta Massina, Fellini's wife, portrays (in one of the screen's most beautiful and most moving performances by a woman) Gelsomina, a retarded girl whose waif-like innocence and smile is, as the sideshow busker and mocked performer, an embodiment of the pathos of the clown.

While so many clowns look idiotic — Dostoevsky's profound clown Prince

Mishkin is called **The Idiot** — they nevertheless often have a wisdom role, challenging the pretences, mirroring the foibles and, along with the mad saviour-figures, able to tell the truth cheekily but truly and be acceptable and accepted. Foolish King Lear, more sinned against than sinning, is privileged to be accompanied in his torment and his tragedy by his discarded daughter Cordelia, his victim-peer Kent, the wronged Edgar pretending to be Poor Tom, and his wise court Fool. Shakespeare gives Lear many clown characters who are agents of grace.

Yet the clown is the object of pathos, the butt of jokes and the teller of jokes, the mocker and the mocked, the artist who creates laughter and the artist who creates tears: poor, little, pathetic — evoking sentiment and compassion. A master of guises and disguises. Send in the clowns! ■

THE RAZOR'S EDGE . . . *Bill Murray as Somerset Maugham's secular saint, Larry Darrell.*

18

Community Builders

In the 'global village'
of easy, almost instant worldwide communication,
community has become important —
in the West with its emphasis on individual fulfilment
and suspicion of socialism
and in the East, more traditionally society-centred.
Figures who are community-builders
are Christ-like.

One of the dangers for those involved in education is focusing too narrowly on individuals and individual development. Commentators say that this is a feature of western cultures. They point to many eastern and Third World cultures where there is a greater emphasis on society and the individual's responsibility and contribution to society, as well as the various social groupings to which the individuals belong. Perhaps western reaction to socialism and communism has made many people too wary of social concern, fearing that it could be interpreted as socialism.

Yet the 20th century is an age of major development in worldwide (and space) communication and in media: entertainment, information, propaganda, for mass audiences. The stress on personalism has also brought a greater awareness of universal humanity and dignity and the need, not just for society, but for community. Community-building, communes, Basic Christian communities and all kinds of group movements have flourished, especially since World War II.

On a global level (the 'global village') we have moved from a League of Nations to the United Nations — a noble ideal, if not always a reality. Common concerns, especially war and the threats of nuclear disaster, have united men and women worldwide.

These tendencies and yearnings echo the deepest Christian longings. The ecumenical movement of our times, echoing Jesus' prayer that all his followers be one, promotes unity instead of division, dialogue instead of polemic (two monologues hurled at each other).

The Second Vatican Council, attuned to the aspirations of the times, highlighted the image of the People of God, the Exodus, journeying Pilgrim People as the principal church symbol (rather than the Mystical Body or the Body of Christ). In fact, the principal document, the Constitution on the Church, has as its title 'The Light of the Nations', indicating the witness value of the People of God as a pledge that God covenants himself with all peoples.

The Old Testament figure of the Servant was the original 'Light of the Nations'. He was presented as an individual, but a symbolic individual, one who was seen to incorporate the ideal features of service: gentle care, consecrated concern, willingness to endure scapegoat hostility, readiness to suffer for others, a Suffering Servant. The Servant was seen as a 'corporate personality': an individual who embodies the qualities of a whole society, who has the power to give meaning and build up society into communion, into community.

It is obvious that the New Testament presents Jesus as this kind of 'corporate personality'. He embodies the best qualities of being human; he is a pledge of his and our Father's covenanting of himself to us; he builds up a 'fellowship of disciples', the kind of community the church ought to be. Examples of what could happen are given in the early chapters of the Acts of the Apostles. It did not, could not, last.

Yet throughout the centuries, many visionaries like St. Augustine have dreamt of building the City of God. It has been seen as the new and heavenly Jerusalem, Heaven or Utopia (which means Nowhere) or Erehwon (which is Nowhere backwards). But the aspiration of city-building brings out the best, even in seemingly unlikely men and women. Community-building is a Christ-like kind of activity.

The Americans have what is called 'The Buddy System'. Australians have 'Mateship'. One of the features of buddies/mates is that one friend, the strong one, is able to support the other in his weakness, the messiness of his life — and not merely once. The weaker friend gains some self-confidence through affirmation, is able to cope and relate more readily and to rejoin the human race. This buddy/mates image is a microcosm of community-building in the wider, often ugly or sleazy world. In the '70s and '80s, this was seen amongst teenagers, especially on the city streets, saving each other: **Foxes, Little Darlings, Times Square.**

Sidney Poitier in many of his films of the '60s took this kind of role: the Lifeline counsellor in **The Slender Thread,** the dedicated teacher in **To Sir With Love,** the friend of the blind girl in **A Patch of Blue.** With humour and sentiment he even transformed a nuns' community as a genial protestant carpenter building a chapel for some German sisters in **Lilies of the Field.**

One of the principal community-building figures of the '70s in films was Billy Jack, the Vietnam veteran, martial arts expert who bridged the world of the white man and the mystical world of red Indian rituals and lore, who stood for the underprivileged against the affluent, the political bullies, the dissolute. He fought physically and by experiencing prison (**Billy Jack**), through legal procedures as well as concern and example (**The Trial of Billy Jack**) and through confrontation of the United States' powers that be (**Billy Jack Goes to Washington** — a remake of the 1939 James Stewart vehicle, **Mr. Smith Goes to Washington**).

The Billy Jack films are strongly tied to the '70s, but they offered a real community-building hero on the screen.

British director Ken Russell, a convert to Catholicism in the '50s, has shown a fascination with offbeat and bizarre Jesus-figures and Christ-figures, especially in **The Devils, Mahler** and **Lisztomania.** But with his often frantic and grotesque evocations of history and composers' lives, he took time to visualise The Who's rock opera, **Tommy.** Tommy emerges as a Christ-figure par excellence, explicitly so. In satire on the emptiness of contemporary religious rituals, on the willingness of crowds to be herded into hysteria and to follow the latest trend, craze or mania, he shows Tommy as the king of pinball, yet a born-again, enlightened Messiah.

Russell and The Who show discipleship gone berserk — but Tommy's leadership had the potential to transform people's lives. The exploiters are always with us and self-proclaimed messianism is bound for destruction. The rock opera's solution is that the true leader is the one who listens like a disciple and can climb the mountain to God. This leader is worth following.

Tommy works on the levels of film entertainment, moral allegory and rock opera — an appeal to the widest communication and community. ■

THE KARATE KID . . . *The engaging Pat Morita trains young Ralph Macchio to grow in more ways than one.*

19

Growth and Transformation

Psychologists and educationists
highlight the dynamic rather than the static
elements of growth.
The emphasis is on **development.**
Figures dramatising growth,
or potential for growth,
are often portrayed as heroes,
saviours or victims.
The films of Richard Gere
are a popular illustration.

Perhaps it was always so, but with the advent of television, then video, with so many adults content to stay at home to imbibe their visual entertainment, cinema since the 1960s seems to have been a medium for younger audiences. Films for children are a significant part of the market. However, the cinema-going public has frequently been identified as 18-25 (perhaps to 30). Many films are specifically geared towards this audience. So too the publicity. So too the types of characters portrayed and the stars (sometimes cult-figures) chosen to embody them.

One of the features to emerge from this is an awareness of the hero and anti-hero (the 'laid-back' or victim or rebel hero) and the saviour/redeemer traits that touch and move the younger audiences.

At the same time, the insights of psychologists have been popularised. Almost everyone is able to draw on some system, aid or, simply, jargon. On a much more serious level, educationists (theoreticians and practitioners) have been applying the fresh insights (especially as they coincide with experience and commonsense) to schooling, family life, to experiences that enable the young to grow.

Developmental Psychology has staked its claim to everyone's attention. I has a powerful effect on religious educationists who are able to speak and write comfortably of stages of faith, growth in appreciation of moral values, participation in the Church's sacraments at appropriate and effective points in life.

The religious educationists, with this developmental perspective, are looking at films and heroes/heroines (anti-heroes/heroines) who dramatise positive growth experiences with Jesus-characteristics. Paul often exhorted his readers to follow Christ 'for their inner selves to grow strong' (Ephesians 3:16).

Once again, the verb 'grow' comes into focus for our being imitators of Paul as he is of God.

Even in the Gospels we see that Jesus 'grew to maturity, and he was filled with wisdom; and God's favour was with him' (Luke 2:40). We see Jesus at the age of 12, his Bar Mitzvah age, so vividly dramatised by Zeffirelli in **Jesus of Nazareth,** a boy on the threshold of adulthood, moving towards a mission in life but, nevertheless, going back to Nazareth from Jerusalem (where he, a reader now of Sacred Scripture in the synagogue, could ask questions of religious leaders). Luke portrays him: 'And Jesus increased in wisdom, in stature and in favour with God and men' (Luke 2:52).

One of the films of the early '80s that appealed to many educationists (though much less to parents) was the Oscar-nominated **An Officer and a Gentleman.** Attention was particularly on the star Richard Gere embodying a character portrayed as growing throughout the film, transformed from a put-upon lout to a genial man with charm and a growing sense of responsibility.

The plot appealed to younger rather than older audiences — who had seen it often before in the **You're In The Navy Now** movies, where raw recruits were given the literal run-around (and more) in rigorous training by a bawling, granite-facaded, mush-hearted sergeant major. In the post-Vietnam U.S., it was popular again in a more permissive and four-letter-word format. But the film evoked intense response and admiration for the Richard Gere character.

The early films of Richard Gere, in fact, offered a star with charisma, energy and qualities for contemporary cinema-goers with appeal for both male and female audiences. Whether Gere, his agent, production companies or publicists noticed this, his eleven starring roles from 1978 to 1987 presented him as the hero/anti-hero developing into a saviour/victim figure.

A brief focus on the use of the Gere persona in each of these films indicates that here is a star (reminiscent of Paul Newman in the '50s and '60s) who is cast as a post-Christian Christ-figure.

• **Days of Heaven:** A misfit young factory-worker, in Chicago 1916, goes West for work and happiness for himself and family, to find it temporarily, but to cause pain and be hounded to death by the police.

• **Blood Brothers:** Chicago 1970s, a sensitive son of a macho-Italian family is forced to labour, fight and 'be a man' by his father; but he relates better to his sickly brother and becomes a warm and successful 'recreation assistant' in a city hospital; he and his brother break out of their oppressive world.

• **Yanks:** A pleasant G.I. stationed in England during World War II meets an English family, loves the daughter — Gere at his most sensitive and tender.

• **American Gigolo:** An American nightmare where a street-wise but naive young man is caught up in affluence and glamour but has to face a deeper self. But it is too late in a world of exploitation and murder.

• **An Officer and a Gentleman:** Your average young man (or a bit below) has the potential to do something with his life by hard work, discipline, selflessness and love — and **be someone.**

- **Breathless:** A frenetic, constantly-moving and agitated con-crook thinks he can beat all the systems, but it is a fantasy that can only end in death — a pop-art gangster anti-hero who sees himself like the Silver Surfer comic-strip saviour he loves. (Gere's pre-star role was as a similarly tense, violent, martial arts bar-prowler, friendly with, using and menacing Diane Keaton's lost, wandering teacher in **Looking for Mr. Goodbar**.)
- **The Honorary Consul:** Richard Gere in Graham Greene-land as a callow young Argentinian doctor who avoids commitment, who sins and betrays, who is asked to help in the social revolution, ultimately learning values and dying futilely to save a friend.

With a film version of Greene, we are in the realm of explicit Christ-figures.

Gere's character dies in three films, is close to death or to violence in the others. The developing Christ-figure is predominantly a figure for younger audiences — and a challenge to older ones.

- **The Cotton Club:** a Prohibition days' saxophone player lives in a gangster atmosphere, escapes danger to emerge as a Hollywood heart-throb star.
- **King David:** a miscast Gere tries to bring dignity to a portrait of David, warrior, dancer before the Lord, sinner, penitent, doting father and leader of his people.
- **Power:** the 1980s up-and-coming man, the media moulder who revels in his power and shrewd manoeuvres, shaping images and designing truth, but who is challenged to integrity.
- **No Mercy:** another police drama, Gere facing the adult exercise of power and conscience-decisions. ■

JENNY'S WAR . . . *War has always been a vivid setting for women to show their strength and compassion. Dyan Cannon is Jenny.*

20

Women as Christ-figures

While there are significant women
in the history of Christianity,
and Scripture offers many themes on the feminine,
women Christ-figures are comparatively rare.
Recent films indicate a change.

Tradition has offered many masculine Christ-figures. While St. Paul emphatically reassures us that amongst the disciples of Jesus there will be no more male and female, this has not always been a keynote of the life of the Church. And yet, in fact, significant women, in the public eye and out of it, have always been important in the Church's development. Their contribution to the discipleship of Jesus has been essential.

It is right that we ask ourselves about women Christ-figures, to highlight the equality of men and women before God.

The New Testament itself highlights with dignity and respect, affection and significance many women, from Jesus' mother Mary to his friends, the sisters Martha and Mary, to disciples, to women healed of illness, of sin. As the Christian communities spread, women martyrs took their place with the men and their courage was exalted in the **Acts of the Martyrs.** In the Middle Ages, if we look at the Church's calendar of feasts, we can note that virgins are particularly honoured. The mothers that are revered are generally royalty.

In the late Middle Ages, and Renaissance period, figures of contradiction appear. Catherine of Siena, an ailing, retiring Dominican tertiary, actually persuaded the Pope to return from Avignon; Joan of Arc led the French to victory against the English. St. Teresa of Avila, from 16th century Spain, has been declared one of **the** learned members of Christianity, a 'Doctor of the Church'.

In more recent centuries, foundresses of religious orders, social worker nuns and, often, visionaries, frequently 'lowly' people, have been spotlit. There have been film portraits of, for example, Joan, Bernadette, Maria Goretti.

The Old Testament has many telling themes focusing on women:

• While Eve is associated with mankind's fall from grace, she is still the mother of all the living. Other women are significant mothers: from Bathsheba to the lovely portrait of the non-Hebrew Ruth. Mary, mother of Jesus, and Elizabeth, her cousin, mother of the Baptist, are in this tradition.

• The very wisdom of God was personified as feminine. In the thinking of the times, the faithful wife was praised in Proverbs 31 as the epitome of Wisdom. Thus, the ideal woman and wisdom are interchangeable.

• Men and women sin. The sinful woman, often the ritual prostitute of pagan fertility rites, was taken as a symbol of the infidelity of Israel, the faithless bride. Yet in the Song of Songs, Israel is the beautiful and loving bride. In the New Testament we find the prostitutes are the very people who change attitude and behaviour because of their treatment by Jesus. Mary Magdalene is the key figure (and it is she who is portrayed both at Calvary and seeking the risen Lord).

• God is also described in feminine imagery:

Does a woman forget her baby at the breast, or fail to cherish the son of her womb? Yet even if these forget, I will never forget you. (Isaiah 49:15).

The same image of giving birth is found in Isaiah 66:9.

• When Jesus came he was seen as the Wisdom of God with its feminine qualities (Heb.1 and Is.6), as a strong and tender man (Mt.11:25-30), and as a man gracious and comfortable with women and men.

Films portraying canonised women saints are an obvious example of feminine Christ-figures. Silent film director Carl Dreyer, whose body of films is explicitly religious, filmed a classic **Passion of Joan of Arc;** Robert Bresson filmed a stark **Trial of Joan of Arc.** Jean Seberg was Joan in Otto Preminger's film of Shaw's play, **Saint Joan.** Ingrid Bergman was a heroic Hollywood crusading figure in **Joan of Arc.**

Jennifer Jones won her Oscar for a portrayal of visionary Bernadette Soubirous, young girl, village eccentric, suffering nun. Italian films have been made of twelve-year-old Maria Goretti and mediaeval repentant prostitute Margaret of Cortona.

Heroic women in Christian service of whatever denomination also qualify easily for feminine Christ-figures. One of the best-known is Ingrid Bergman's picture of Gladys Aylward and her work in China in **The Inn of the Sixth Happiness.** (A tough variation on this picture of Christian women in China is John Ford's offbeat **Seven Women.**) There are many pictures of nuns, many pious and/or sentimental, many vigorous and compelling. **Conspiracy of Hearts** shows a more ecumenical picture as Italian nuns, with Lilli Palmer as Superior, hide and shelter Jewish orphans during World War II.

In the '50s there were many tributes to heroic groups and individuals and their World War II exploits. Again, women, prepared to suffer and give their lives for causes or for fellow human beings, received attention. Fine examples include Anna Neagle as **Odette** and Virginia McKenna as Violette Szabo in **Carve Her Name With Pride.** Virginia McKenna also appeared in the Japanese prison-camp drama **A Town Like Alice.** In the '70s the Billy Graham organisation filmed Corrie ten Boom's **The Hiding Place** with its memories of **The Diary of Anne Frank;** there was the moving telemovie **Playing for Time** with Vanessa Redgrave and Jane Alexander. Meryl Streep also suffered in **Sophie's Choice.**

One of the most moving feminine Christ-figures is Harriet Andersson's Agnes in Ingmar Bergman's superb **Cries and Whispers.** She is seriously ill and has a harrowing death scene. Her death affects her proud and selfish sisters and her maid who, like an earth mother, cradles her corpse as a dead Christ in Pietà-fashion. The minister at her burial speaks of her in Christ terms. He then goes on to explain the significance of her life:

*"If it is so that you have gathered our suffering in your poor body, if it is so that you have borne it with you through death, if it is so that you meet God over there in the other land, if it is so that He turns His face toward you, if it is so that you can speak the language that this God understands, if it is so that you can, then speak to this God. If it is so, pray for us ... Pray for us who are left here on the dark, dirty earth under an empty and cruel Heaven. Lay your burden of suffering at God's feet and ask Him to pardon us. Ask Him to free us at last from our anxiety, our weariness and our deep doubt. Ask Him for a meaning to our lives. Agnes, you who have suffered so unimaginably and so long, **you must be worthy to plead our cause.**"*

This is Christ-figure symbolism at its best.

A delightful variation is the Gelfling Kira in Jim Henson's **The Dark Crystal.** In Henson's fantasy, redemption (universal and personal harmony) can be achieved by the masculine and feminine working together. In **The Dark Crystal,** the male Gelfling performs the saving action; but he can do it only because of the sacrifice of her life by Kira. She is then loved into new life by Jen (a trait in early '80s science fiction, where wives love their experimenting scientist-husbands away from death: **Altered States, Brainstorm**).

Feminine Christ-figures are a contemporary creative challenge. ■

WATERSHIP DOWN . . . *Rabbits as saviour-figures? Animated version of Richard Adam's fable.*

21

Off-beat Christ-figures

Jesus was seen in New Testament times
as the Lamb of God.
Symbols were used to evoke
his memory and presence.
Recently, less obvious figures resembling Christ
have been seen on screen.

There are several 'characters' in films that have been identified as Christ-figures but sometimes cause hesitancy: some of them are not human. 'Off-beat' is a useful term for those characters, human or not, who are not so immediately obvious as Christ-figures.

When we look back at Scripture and the use of signs and symbols of the early Church, we realise it is traditional enough to use the imagination for symbols of Jesus. The Book of Isaiah highlighted the Servant of Yahweh as 'led like a lamb to the slaughter', bearing our sins for us. Old Testament writers often played on words — there is only one letter difference for lamb (ebed) and servant (eben) in Hebrew.

By the Gospel times and, especially the poetic book of Revelation, Jesus could be referred to as the Lamb of God, and John portrayed Jesus as dying at the moment the Passover lambs were killed in the temple. Liturgy and Christian art perpetuated the figure of the Lamb.

The early followers of Jesus also used 'baptised' Roman and Greek emblems: the mythical Phoenix which rose from its ashes signified the Resurrection; Jesus, the 'Sun of Justice' was like Apollo in his chariot. The Christians also used the fish sign with its Greek letters ICHTHUS, the initials of Jesus Christ, Son of God, Saviour.

There is a famous piece of Roman Empire graffiti where schoolboys drew the head of a donkey on a crucified figure to mock Christ.

There are precedents for the off-beat Christ-figures.

With J. R. Tolkien and the many contemporary fantasy-writers, the age-old legends and myths are being re-worked and re-set in an imaginary past or a science-fiction present or a fantasy future. The popular, even comic-book Christ-figures are at home in these worlds. But Tolkien created a different world, different creatures. Frodo, the Hobbitt, has become a universal favourite as he and his companions, aided by the wizard father-figure Gandolf, go in quest of the Rings. U.S. animator Ralph Bahkshi ventured into visualising these characters in a film dramatising the first part of this saga.

Muppets' creator Jim Henson followed the Tolkien lead with **The Dark Crystal,** set in a different world with new creatures. Influenced by myths and C. G. Jung, Henson's world needs redemption because it has been shattered. The good side of life and the evil side have separate existences. Two surviving creatures, Gelflings — male and female and childlike — have the task of finding the shard missing from the dark crystal and restoring it at a special time so that peace and harmony can be restored. Hero Jen replaces the shard but can do so only because heroine Kira has been willing to sacrifice her life. If the story of Jesus is 'archetypal', the age-old and universal story of evil and grace, these fantasies are Christ-figure stories.

The same thing is evident in some popular animal fables of the '70s: the animated film of Richard Adams' **Watership Down** and the blend of realism and stylised live action of Richard Bach's **Jonathan Livingston Seagull.**

Watership Down takes the mythic form of a journey and a quest. However, the setting is linked to contemporary human problems of conservation, exploitation of the land, abuses of technology and growth and the need for a purer life-style, more harmonious with nature rather than a Tolkien 'eucatastrophe', where a great disaster and suffering lead to universal harmony. The theme of **Watership Down** is reminiscent of Max Fleischer's 1942 animated **Hoppity Goes to Town** and the 1981 **Secret of Nimh.** Hazel, the rabbit who leads the group to safety, not without struggle and suffering, is, of course, the saviour-figure.

Jonathan Livingston Seagull is not specifically Christian. Readers see Buddhist influences and, in fact, the book and film (aided by Neil Diamond's very popular score with its religious, poetic lyrics) have been seen as a fable of the human condition, the human struggle, religious experience and self-transcendence.

A creative fable about the human condition is austere French Catholic Robert Bresson's **Au Hazard, Balthazar,** a story of French provincial life in the '60s, of farms, town activities, gangs, violence and seduction, circuses and alpine smuggling — a recognisable world of good and evil. However, Balthazar is a donkey. His life of joy but, more, of suffering intertwines with that of a young girl, Marie. The film is full of Gospel and Christian tradition references and allusions. Bresson has deliberately not made an allegory but offers, he says, echoes for depth and for resonance with the life and suffering of Christ. Bresson's French sensibility, subtlety and style make this film more acceptable and plausible than it might otherwise have been.

Jesus was crucified between two thieves, condemned as a criminal. The image of the suffering Jesus of the Crucifix, mocked and beaten, stripped, hanging nailed, is that of a criminal. Jesus was taken by watchers as a criminal.

In Bryan Forbes' **Whistle Down the Wind** a criminal is taken for Jesus. Three children hear an escaped murderer, Alan Bates, swear 'Jesus Christ' and take it that he is Jesus. As the children bring him gifts and reverence him, ultimately defying authority to save him, Alan Bates is photographed more and more in Christ profiles and postures and with an aura around him. The children's faith in this Jesus, jolted at times but resilient, is contrasted with that of an ineffectual vicar, preaching theoretical Christian charity and Sunday school religion.

While the film may be seen as a parable of the coming of Christ and mankind's response to him (God revealed, not to the learned and the clever but to mere children: Mt.11), it could also be seen as an attack on mistaken, childish, wishful-thinking belief in Christ.

At the end, as the murderer is captured, the photography and screen composition have overtones of the crucifixion.

In a period of growing interest in and acceptance of symbolism, fantasy, psychological insights and a theology of story, we might expect a growing number of off-beat Christ-figures. ■

HAMLET . . . *Nicol Williamson plays the hero-victim, mad 'north by northwest'; with Ophelia (Marianne Faithfull).*

22

Mad Saviours

Jesus was accused of being mad.
Paul knew that God's madness
is greater than human wisdom.
Truth is often told in madness —
by the insane as well as by the very simple.

'Madness' is quite an arbitrary term. People, ideas, words, plans can all be derided as 'mad'. The word can be used in insult, in amazement. Madness can, more seriously, be seen as a kind of death, a loss of ordinary life and opportunity as people 'lose their minds'. This kind of madness is feared, covered over as the insane are removed from society, often for their own and others' protection.

Sanity and madness cannot be strictly defined. Norms establishing a so-called healthy state of mind are based on tradition and community expectations. These are not always clearly understood or administered, with the result that history shows us many innocent victims of society's judgements. However, several cultures have thought the mad to be possessed by strange spirits and thus given special powers — of knowledge, insight, of healing, of magic.

It is not surprising that in literature and drama, the mad have often been made oracular utterers of truth.

Jesus was accused of being mad, of being possessed. So were his earliest disciples. Through the centuries, many of Jesus' disciples have been mocked, persecuted, cast out and killed as mad men, mad women. The Gospels tell us that Jesus' own family thought that he was mad (Mark 3:21); the religious leaders said that the Devil himself had hold of Jesus and this was the only way that he had control over evil spirits (Luke 11:15). As the leaders also mocked Jesus dying on the cross, they taunted him with acting in an insane way (Mt.27:39-43).

Paul was able to sum up this confusion, this mystery of vision and idiocy as important for his spirituality:

If it was God's wisdom that human wisdom should not know God, it was because God wanted to save those who have faith through the foolishness of the message that we preach. And so, while the Jews demand miracles and the Greeks look for wisdom, here are we preaching a crucified Christ; to the Jews an obstacle that they cannot get over, to the pagans madness, but to those who have been called, whether they are Jews or Greeks, a Christ who is the power and wisdom of God (1 Cor.1:21-25)

Paul here emphasises the value of foolishness.

Another Gospel phrase used of Jesus (by Simeon to Mary in Luke 2:34-35) is 'Sign of Contradiction'. The fool-figure is always such a sign. There is truth told in madness.

A classic dramatising of this is in the central storm scenes of **King Lear.** Lear has acted foolishly in believing the adulation of money-grasping daughters and exiling the daughter who loved him. Cast out by scorn and ingratitude, he storms as a tempest rages; he loses his balance and sanity. It is only his court fool, with the noble exiled Kent in disguise and the victim son, Edgar, impersonating a madman, Poor Tom, who can comfort Lear and speak any truth to him.

The trappings and behaviour of the mad may be bizarre; their words often ring strangely true.

There is a caution in considering madness. Often it is destructive. The fanaticism of those who 'play God', who persecute, not only in the name of Christ, but where the inquisitor, for instance, claims the authority of Christ himself, has been appalling over the centuries. Opposing armies are blessed in the name of God and slaughter and havoc wreaked 'for his glory'. It is a commonplace that many confined to asylums identify themselves with Jesus and claim to be Christ.

A powerful film which captures this mania and fanaticism in the name of Jesus is John Houston's version of Flannery O'Connor's **Wise Blood.** Set in U.S. Revivalist territory, the film shows the passion and death of Hazel Motes, a grandson of a hellfire preacher, who rebels against religion, declares that he does not believe in sin or redemption and tries to prove it. His preaching ability leads him to proclaim a Church Without Christ — encountering an allegedly blind preaching conman and his wilful daughter, Sabbath Lily, and a huckster of religions. He also gains a disciple, the innocent Enoch Emery. But Hazel, still tormented by his sense of sin, blinds and tortures himself and runs away to die.

The Jesus parallel is real but obsessively misguided and self-destructive.

A savage, yet blackly hilarious film dramatising these themes is **The Ruling Class.** It attacks the pompous, arrogant and decaying traditions of British aristocracy and its faith in its God and itself. Included in the lampooning is the established Church, personified by a comic-doddering Alistair Sim as a bishop, unable to kneel, bullied by the ruling class and incapable of perceiving genuine religious insight. Peter O'Toole is Jack, the heir, who believes himself to be God, dresses as Jesus, always answering to divine names. He preaches a gospel of love, even spending time suspended on a cross in his drawing-room. A lot of wisdom and genuine religion is spoken by the madman.

A psychologist confronts Jack with another man who believes himself to be God and who displays his psychic power as the Electric Messiah. Jack is defeated — appears to be normal again, but has moved to a new interior identity, new murdering behaviour as Jack the Ripper. In its complexities, **The Ruling Class,** full of bravura acting and visuals, shows the wise folly of God as the sadistic madness of violence.

In a much gentler vein, Peter O'Toole also portrayed the classic madman who went about doing good: Don Quixote. In **Man of La Mancha,** the authors identify Miguel Cervantes, imprisoned by the Inquisition, with his character, the Don. Beauty is in the eye of the beholder, we say, but some eyes can see the inner beauty and be catalysts for its emergence. With the rituals and symbolism of chivalry, Don Quixote, the Knight of the Woeful Countenance, sees a draught horse as a noble steed, a girl at a village inn as the Lady Dulcinea and while he tilts at windmills, he engages battle with evil and dreams impossible dreams.

Many of those judged mad are, in scriptural terms, 'wise' with the simplicity of doves. They show the childlike face of Jesus, especially against evil, showing it up in its ugliness and destructiveness. Boo Radley, the gentle recluse of **To Kill A Mockingbird** and the similar Snowman, the albino tried for murder in **When Every Day was the Fourth of July,** are fine examples.

American films of buddies show the physically strong but mentally weak friend and the smart friend who gives up his ambitions to help and save the companion. John Steinbeck's **Of Mice and Men** is the classic presentation. An adaptation to the squalid streets of New York were the characters Joe Buck and Ratso Rizzo in **Midnight Cowboy.** 'As long as you did it to the least of my brothers, you did it to me.'

> *... It was to shame the wise that God chose what is foolish by human reckoning, and to shame what is strong that he chose what is weak by human reckoning; those whom the world thinks common and contemptible are the ones that God has chosen — those who are nothing at all to show up those who have everything (1 Cor 1:27-28).* ■

WHOLLY MOSES . . . *Dudley Moore is a Moses-figure in this film, part of the spate of biblical spoofs of which* The Life of Brian *is the best-known.*

23

Satiric Figures, Savage Moralists

Satire is not the easiest entertainment.
Sometimes bleak, sometimes black,
it often goes 'over the top'
and quickly offends.
Yet satirists are savage moralists
with high expectations of society.
Religion is a butt of satire —
sometimes by the use of ironic Christ-parallels.

In a brief letter to the editor of a Melbourne daily paper, the correspondent complained about the immorality of nudity. The paper's cartoonist had an accompanying visual comment: Jesus on the cross in a suit and tie. Most people enjoy irony and declare a faith in a sense of humour. It has been said that anything that cannot be laughed at is an **idol.** But, while we may all agree that we should be able to laugh, we disapprove of humorous presentations that are in bad taste or offensive.

And yet . . . the dictum about one man's food being another man's poison is true of humour and, especially, of satire.

Satire has always played an important role as a moderator of the excesses of human enthusiasm and righteousness. It is a corrective to the foibles humankind is always manifesting. But it is a corrective and comment at the other extreme — we know that a short, sharp, exaggerated stab can often bring home the point of a major issue.

In satire the human situation is exaggerated and laughed at. The audience is made to laugh **at** people and situations rather than **with** them. The point is dissatisfaction with the current situation and values. An attempt is made in satirical films to show the futility of treating stupid humans seriously; the satire may go on to search out ways for a solution or, at least, of bettering the situation. Laughing at or ridiculing the values of a society which takes itself too seriously is one of the obvious trends in satirical films today.

Satire is obviously (though not so obviously to those who prefer their humour plain, direct and less subtle) a partial view of the world, highlighting values by their absence. Satirists are dissatisfied with the world. They know there ought to be something better. They also know that some people are blind to this unless their complacency in the **status quo** is shattered. Satirists, despite appearances to the contrary, are savage perfectionists and moralists.

Since the early '60s, with the first major nuclear confrontations and the worldwide protests and questioning of traditional values, satire has been referred to as black comedy. As Stanley Kramer's comedy of the time said **It's a Mad Mad Mad Mad World.**

Black comedy:

- sets up a world and attacks it
- uses irony to poke fun
- uses exaggerations
- is not wary of 'excess' and is prepared to go 'over the top'
- breaks through limits of subject and 'good taste'
- intends to offend.

Film directors from whom audiences have come to expect satire in religious matters include Ken Russell (the fantasies of **Mahler** and his conversion from Judaism to Catholicism, the living cartoon effects and illustrations of **Lizstomania**) and Federico Fellini (his **Roma,** the religious school plays of **Juliet of the Spirits**). Even a devout Catholic director like Ermanno Olmi can give a critical version of the Magi's journey (many anti-clerical touches) in **Cammina Cammina (Keep on Walking).**

The Monty Python comedians have used satire on religion. In **The Meaning of Life** their musical comedy routine (more than reminiscent of **Oliver**), 'Every Sperm is Sacred' is a barbed spoof on Catholic moral teaching on birth control. No sooner is it over than a couple who have been watching the musical spectacle are revealed as bigoted, free-thinking, puritan-practical Protestants. Ultimately Heaven is shown as a Las Vegas casino floor-show with a star crooner (more than reminiscent of Jack Jones or Engelbert Humperdinck).

But the Python's best-known satire on religion was **The Life of Brian.** Many American audiences, perhaps puzzled by the subtleties of Flying Circus humour, as well as not wanting the Gospel stories to be associated with irreverent humour, reacted in a strongly hostile manner. English and Australian audiences responded favourably and with laughter. **The Life of Brian** is not a satire on Jesus himself but rather on institutional religion, on indiscriminate longing for a Messiah. It also satirises the cinema 'epic' traditions of biblical and Roman movies. The film gibes at unions, revolution, feminism and other contemporary targets.

However, Brian's life parallels the well-known life of Jesus in many respects — Brian is definitely a satiric Christ-figure. One remembers that Jesus fled people who mistook his kingdom as 'of this world' and wanted to make him king. Brian is most unwilling to be chosen as Messiah — and, as he escapes, he drops his gourd and loses a shoe. Followers find each and immediately factional discipleship ('his gourd,' 'his shoe') erupts into violent clash. Obviously, the Pythons sail close to the wind at times, but **Brian** is the best example of the satiric Christ-figure.

Another area of satire on religion in films is the presentation of evangelists (generally American). Films include **Elmer Gantry, Angel Baby, Day of the**

Locusts, The Disappearance of Aimee. Marty Feldman wrote, directed and starred in a satire on modern television evangelists, **In God We Trust.** It has many funny moments and lines ('God gave us his son at Christmas. What are you going to give God? ... It's not the thought that counts, it's the gift ... The bucks stop here') but was a critical and box office failure. Feldman himself played an innocent monk who is sent out into the world to find funds for the monastery and gets caught up in the world of religious wheeler-dealers and kind prostitutes.

One of the most effective satiric Christ-figures appears in Pier Paolo Pasolini's short episode in **Rogopag.** Called **The Cream Cheese,** it was a satire on the filming of a biblical spectacular on a Roman hillside. The scene was the Crucifixion. The actors who posed for the typical baroque Pietà tableau could not have cared less about religion or Christ as they fooled about waiting for filming. They had even less regard for Christ's counterparts, the needy poor of Rome around them. The hungry poor man who plays the good thief eventually steals a poodle belonging to an actress and with the money buys bread and a cream cheese with which he stuffs himself.

The scene is to be filmed in view of Roman celebrities and the press. He rehearses his lines, 'Lord, remember me when you come into your kingdom' and the answer of Christ, 'This day you will be with me in Paradise'. After wolfing his food so greedily, waiting on the cross for the visitors to finish cocktails is too much for Cicco, the hero, and he dies. The director, played by Orson Welles, turns to the camera and remarks, 'Poor Cicco, he had to die before we even knew he was alive'. This is a biblical message. ■

THE SIMPLE-MINDED MURDERER . . . *A young Swedish man has visions of angels and becomes an avenger.*

24

Angels on Screen: Protective Messengers

Angels are mediators between God and mankind.
They manifest the special presence of God,
personify him, communicate his message.
They have been seen as guardians, as avengers.

In many religions, God seems so remote from his worshippers that they feel a need to bridge the distance between deity and humanity. They long for a mediator. In the Old Testament, the First Commandment forbade images of Yahweh. He was a living, a spiritual God. In his dealings with the Hebrew people, he acted towards and was experienced by such figures as Abraham, Moses, Samuel directly. However, the tradition developed a way of speaking about the interaction of God and mankind. It was through Messengers of God. From the Greek word for messenger, we have the word 'angel'.

Angels were seen as aspects of God himself. The language for and images of angels derived from the language and images of religious experience and stories of the time. Very human travelling angels visit Sodom before its destruction (Genesis 18), a reassuring angel speaks to the mothers of the judges Gideon and Samson. Majestic attendants at Yahweh's court in the Jerusalem temple take tongs from a sacred fire to cleanse the lips of the prophet Isaiah (Isaiah 6).

Later, when the Chosen People experienced exile in Babylon, they saw the images of divine or exalted beings, creatures with multiple qualities represented in the statuary: human head for intelligence, lion's body for strength, eagle's wings to soar. The prophet Ezekiel saw a complex vision like this and described it as 'something like the glory of Yahweh' (Ezekiel 1).

In later centuries before the coming of Christ, under the influence of images and stories from Babylon and the East, a whole system was developed: choirs of angels in a hierarchy of groups, names and characteristics of particular messengers who were close to God and received important commissions for dealing with mankind — Raphael the healer, Gabriel the announcer of the final times, Michael the confronter of evil.

This was the background to the New Testament where the presence and activity of angels is taken for granted — the Old Testament allusions and meaning, the world-view, developed by Paul and the early Church, where angels were spirits, spiritual creatures below God, above humanity. In the book of Revelation (as in the Old Testament book of Daniel), they are more particularly associated with the end of the world than with the heavenly court.

Other ways of speaking of God's dealings with the world were developed in the Old Testament traditions and literature. There was the creative 'Breath of God' of Genesis, the Spirit of God that seized prophets, the Word of God, so powerful that it achieved what it said. These were **personifications** of God.

As the Old Testament came to an end, these aspects of God were spoken of more personally. They became **personalisations.** The time was ripe for the coming of Jesus as the Word of God.

It can be seen that the development of awareness of the messengers, angels, of Yahweh and the greater personalising of Yahweh's qualities are interlinked. There is a strong New Testament association between Jesus and angels.

As with the visualising of Jesus and the mysteries of faith, so there have been great changes in the artistic representation of angels. The solemn court attendants of the Byzantine mosaics contrast with the mediaeval instrument-players of Italian frescoes and the fatty infant cherubs of the Renaissance. The 19th century softened the images to a devotional piety and holy card kitsch, discreet ladylike figures in shapeless nighties, tender guardian angels. The early cinema inherited these images — and, of course, linked them with the sounds of music of the alleged heavenly choirs.

Angels have been consistently popular on screen. Attempts have been made to dramatise biblical episodes. The easiest way has been to use a combination of actor, bright light, unearthly voice, chords, strings and choir. Two interesting interpretations of angels as God's mysterious messengers are found in John Huston's **The Bible** and Franco Zeffirelli's **Jesus of Nazareth.**

In the former, Peter O'Toole plays the three angels who come to warn Sodom. In any scene, the face of only one angel is visible, the other two hooded and averted. But the visible faces vary from scene to scene — earthly and unearthly.

Zeffirelli's version of the annunciation to Mary opts for a 'presence' and a sense of God acting rather than the literal visualising of an angel. The effect, which works very well, is obtained by suggestion, light (shining and reflected from Mary) and sound.

Angel-messengers in popular films warn people about their lives or indicate that death is at hand and good deeds have to be done. In Marc Connolly's popular all-black drama **Green Pastures,** 'De Lawd' and his messengers were portrayed in simple biblical style. Straight-faced comedian Jack Benny had an 'end is at hand' mission in **The Horn Blows at Midnight.**

Even in the '80s in **Two of a Kind,** John Travolta was given a chance to show his love for and save Olivia Newton-John by a fluorescent-suffused group of angels led by Charles Durning and Beatrice Straight against Oliver Reed's dapper and portly Devil. Fortunately these angels materialised in fairly workaday fashion and dress from time to time.

In fact, many of the screen's angels are guardian angels — generally in comedies with the lightest of supernatural touches: protecting baseballers in

Angels in the Outfield; they sound benign or acerbic like Edmund Gwenn and Clifton Webb in **For Heaven's Sake.**

One of the most delightful guardians is Henry Travers in Frank Capra's warm story of post-war America, **It's a Wonderful Life.** Entirely different, and one of the most powerful of angel-figures, are the angels in the Swedish **The Simple-Minded Murderer.** A young worker, ridiculed because of harelip and his seeming a simpleton, reads the Bible, especially the book of Revelation. As he reads, he hears Verdi's Requiem and sees huge, strong angels, statuesque with giant wing-span. Ultimately they accompany him to kill the evil and oppressive master of a factory. These are the apocalyptic, the avenging angels. ∎

THE MISSION . . . *Daniel Berrigan, SJ, peace activist, as Fr. Sebastian, with Jeremy Irons as the saintly missionary, Fr. Gabriel, in Robert Bolt's story of a South American mission tragedy.*

25

Saints as Christ-figures

Saints, by definition, are holy.
They are never self-canonised.
Their following of Christ,
their becoming Christ-figures,
is God's doing
and affirmed by popular acclamation.
It is almost inevitable
that films be made of their lives,
and that they be treated reverentially
and as larger than life.

Saints are the men and women publicly acknowledged as Christ-figures. In the Catholic tradition, saints were popularly acclaimed as such until the early Middle Ages. Their official recognition, their being put on the lists of the saints was called 'canonisation'.

During the Middle Ages, then with tighter controls from the 18th century onwards, ecclesiastical processes were set up: investigations of life and writings, honours paid by the faithful to the candidate for sainthood, miraculous interventions by God at the intercession of the saint.

As in life, so in death, it is no easy thing to be a saint.

However, the New Testament call to all disciples of Christ is to holiness. Paul frequently exhorts those to whom he writes to 'be imitators of me as I am of Christ', to 'be imitators of God'. The pattern of Jesus' life and his relationship to God, his father, is the pattern of Christian holiness.

Paul addresses the early Christian communities as 'saints' and prays blessings of holiness on them. He writes in the vein of the Old Testament book of Daniel where those who remain faithful are called 'the people of the saints of the Most High' who come into the presence of God to receive their reward. The book of Revelation frequently portrays this heavenly court of saints in picturesque symbolic language.

More concretely, the New Testament offers many individuals whose following of Christ singles them out as saints — but whose way of acting is able to be imitated and is not beyond the reach of fellow Christians. The apostles were prompt in following Jesus but, obviously, were by no means perfect. Their heroism comes after a long 'apprenticeship' and their being filled with the Spirit at Pentecost.

Martha and Mary are hospitable, devoted to Jesus (Lk.10) but presented also as women of deep faith when their brother Lazarus dies (Jn.11). The Acts of the Apostles is filled with 'saints' whose ministry is characterised by Paul: for instance, prophets, evangelists, pastors, teachers (Ephesians 4:11).

While saints might be the last to proclaim themselves such, they soon receive the halo, pedestal and niche treatment. Piety prevails. This is often the tone of the films made about them, sometimes little more than animated holy cards relying on the edifying remark, the pious posture backed by celestial choirs.

As with the early cinema Jesus-figures, 19th century religious art and the sentimental stereotypes influenced the film-makers and reinforced audience expectations. While intending to do good, such portraits do harm, alienating those repelled by the sugary sanctity. They receive ambiguous responses from audiences who, while liking the films, feel that the lives of the saints are remote from everyday living and that holiness is unattainable.

Commentators note that the two saints most frequently given screen treatment are Francis of Assisi and Joan of Arc.

Francis of Assisi has been an all-time favourite with all Christian denominations. Three films on him illustrate changing styles and tastes. In 1951 Italian director Roberto Rossellini dramatised the legends associated with Francis, the book called 'The Little Flowers of St. Francis'. The black and white style was a blend of late '40s 'neo-realism' and picturesquely pious sentiment. In the late '50s, Hollywood went to authentic locations in Assisi and Perugia with Cinemascope and colour for a more down-to-earth treatment with Bradford Dillman and Dolores Hart as Francis and Clare. Warfare, papal court, Muslim sultans added drama.

In the early '70s, Franco Zeffirelli directed a typically beautiful portrait of youthful zest, protest and piety in exquisite colours and settings accompanied by Donovan's songs, **Brother Sun, Sister Moon.** In these twenty years there was a transition from gentle reverence to attempted realism to mediaeval symbols relevant to the changes in society and religious belief and commitment of the '60s.

An old-fashioned style '60s portrait of a levitating Franciscan saint who miraculously passed exams to be ordained, Joseph of Cupertino, was **The Reluctant Saint** with Maximilian Schell.

A saint whose ministry to galley-slaves and the Paris poor, as well as to the King of France and his court, has been remembered since the 17th century is St. Vincent de Paul, who was well served in the Oscar-winning and popular French film of 1948, **Monsieur Vincent.**

European directors have made several films of the lives of saints who were well-known locally: St. Margaret of Cortona, St. Maria Goretti. But films about Joan of Arc and Bernadette are best-known to English-speaking audiences. Great directors Carl Theodore Dreyer, 1928, and Robert Bresson, 1962, made stark versions of Joan's **Trial** (Bresson) and **Passion** (Dreyer).

In the United States as early as 1917 Cecil B. de Mille had made a spectacle of Joan with celebrated opera star of the period, Geraldine Farrar. Thirty years later Ingrid Bergman saw herself as the warrior-maid and martyr in **Joan of Arc.** This was based on a play by Maxwell Anderson. In 1957, Otto Preminger chose the unknown young Jean Seberg to be **Saint Joan** in his star-cast version of George Bernard Shaw's play.

On screen Joan has seemed a credible saint when treated straightforwardly rather than spectacularly.

Jennifer Jones won an Oscar as Bernadette Soubirous in **The Song of Bernadette** (1943) where sincerity was mixed with sentiment, war feeling, fascination with the Lourdes story and miracles, good acting and popular conceptions of what saints were supposed to be like, especially when harsh treatment and suffering followed gifts of grace.

Perhaps the most successful film of a saint's life is Fred Zinnemann's multi-award-winning version of Robert Bolt's portrait of Thomas More, **A Man for All Seasons** (1966). As portrayed by Paul Scofield he is the statesman, the family man, the man of wit, charm and conviction and a man of faith. An intelligent pageant, the film was released soon after Richard Burton's portrait of **Becket** in the adaptation of Jean Anouilh's play.

These fine films, while they offered 'men for all seasons', did not offer us the lives of everyday people.

We have an innate desire for heroes and heroines. We seem to be driven to hero-worship, happy to look up at the celebrity on the pedestal. It has happened to the saints and their lives are dramatised accordingly, whether we like it or not. ■

THE DEVILS . . . *Oliver Reed as the worldly priest, Grandier, becomes a martyr to conscience and political expediency.*

26

Movie Priests and Nuns

Dramatists and screenwriters,
whatever their religious background or affiliation,
have been fascinated by priests and nuns.
Cinema traditions have meant
an over-pious treatment.
Critique and caricature have been prominent.
Yet the priest as 'another Christ'
is one of the clearest of the Christ-figures.

Since the early decades of the Church, the priest has been considered as 'alter Christus', 'another Christ'. The priest, has always been a Christ-figure. At times, the dignity of the priesthood meant that the priest was seen as an exalted figure, another Christ mirroring the 'anointed one', singled out to represent humankind in its dealings with God, especially in ritual worship.

At other times, the focus has been on the priest's ministry. He is another Christ who should come to serve rather than be served. Both dignity and ministry have always been considered in the language of ideals. They were to be seen fully in the person of Jesus.

Because the ideal can never be achieved in any individual priest, the sins of the priest, the priest-failure, has always held a fascination for writers and dramatists. The counterpoint between Jesus-ideal and priest-sinner offers creative possibilities for perceiving Jesus himself through his priestly Christ-figures.

It is easy to see in films about world religions or religions of the past that the priest has been considered a consecrated man, set apart, the recipient of a sacred power and authority for leadership, for mediation between the community and its God and for worship. Morris West has explored this in the language of Pacific religions paralleling Christianity in his novel, 'The Navigator'.

Current discussion concerning women in the priesthood has heightened awareness of the role of women in ministry. Traditionally (and the film industry relies heavily on the traditions), the woman in Christian ministry has been the nun. For most of the Church's history the nuns have been dedicated women living an enclosed community life. The emphasis has been on a contemplative style and the detail of convent routine. The 19th and 20th centuries have seen nuns moving to all fields of ministry, from the hospitals and schools to social work, administration and missionary activity in the Third World.

As with cinema presentations of Jesus, 19th century iconography and art styles have meant that movie priests and nuns have been frequently presented as 'too good to be true'. 'Holy' poses and gestures, words that seem sanctimonious rather than saintly, quaint or somewhat ridiculously other-worldly have been the characteristics of clergy and nuns.

Mother Superiors, parish priests (often Irish) and bishops have had authority (or authoritarianism) thrust upon them with the result that for an audience that has little knowledge of Christianity or the Church, clerical movie-figures are cyphers or caricatures.

In an age when satire is acceptable and needed, such figures are obvious targets for highlighting the inadequacy of religion and the Church. Writers and directors from Catholic countries often react ironically against the established Church. Luis Bunuel's **L'Age D'Or** has skeletal and statuesque bishops portraying dressed-up dead religion. **Nazarin** is Bunuel's ideal priest, Christ-like in service but attacked by authority. The episcopal and papal pageant designed as a mock-ecclesiastical fashion show is a startlingly comic critique in Fellini's **Roma.**

But it is not only the established Catholic Church that receives such attack. Alistair Sim's bishop in **The Ruling Class** or Peter Sellers' minister in **Heavens Above** are Anglican butts. The cruel and self-righteous bishop in Ingmar Bergman's **Fanny and Alexander** is a graphic indictment of severe Reformed religion.

While so many actresses have been eager to play nuns — Ingrid Bergman, Deborah Kerr, Claudette Colbert, Rosalind Russell — there have been a number of significant films exploring this religious vocation. **The Song of Bernadette** focused on a peasant girl's visions, but much of it concerned her struggles with her Novice Mistress. This harsh aspect of religious commitment and the system was explored in two films based on Rumer Godden's novels: Anglican sisters in India, **Black Narcissus,** and Catholic Benedictines in **In This House of Brede.**

The best-known film on convent life and vocational choices is Fred Zinnemann's **The Nun's Story** with Audrey Hepburn. War stories, school stories, hospital stories abound — everybody seems to have seen **Heaven Knows, Mr Allison.** In the '60s even, Stella Stevens showed the effect of Vatican II on changes of religious habit and nuns' participation in protests — **Where Angels Go, Trouble Follows.**

By the '80s, a film like **Choices of the Heart** on lay workers and nuns in contemporary clothes, and at work in El Salvador, can show Archbishop Romero and the missionaries being assassinated.

The range of priests presented on screen is wide:

● Hail-fellow well-met. Perhaps the most popular has been Bing Crosby in **Going My Way** — warm, humorous, sentimental, common-sense.

● Good pastors. These are seen, especially in biographies of clergymen like Norman Vincent Peale (**One Man's Way**), Peter Marshall (**A Man Called Peter**), as men of obvious sincerity.

● Burly crusaders. From Spencer Tracy in the **Boys' Town** films to Karl Malden in **On The Waterfront.** These are men of social concern who know God is with them.

- Pastors in critical situations. Early Gregory Peck in **The Keys of the Kingdom** or late Gregory Peck as the Scarlet Pimpernel of the Vatican in **The Scarlet and the Black;** or in moving Italian films like Aldo Fabrizzi in **Open City.**
- Stars of melodrama, soap opera. Best-known is Tom Tryon as **The Cardinal;** later there was Christopher Reeve as **Monsignor.**
- Men of strength and sinfulness. The hero of the various versions of **The Power and the Glory;** Robert de Niro as the Los Angeles Archdiocesan Chancellor in **True Confessions.**
- Tormented men, especially by celibacy. Charles Boyer in **The Garden of Allah,** the puritanical missionary of Somerset Maugham's **Rain, Miss Sadie Thompson;** or tormented by faith doubts: the pastor in Ingmar Bergman's **Winter Lights.**
- The caricature. He is the ineffectual support, the hand-wringing moralist, the platitudinous adviser, the remote commander, the plastic or unctuous hand-shaker — who has appeared in a myriad of films.

The presentation of priests on the screen has often been with an eye to the box-office or with the aim of being critical of religion or of religious men and women. There have been many impressive characterisations, however, which do highlight the fact that Christ-like heroism, even in sinful men and women, can be achieved. ■

SAVING GRACE . . . *The friendly stranger in the Calabrian village (Tom Conti) is actually the Pope working with the poor.*

27

Good and Evil Strangers

We are contradictions to ourselves,
sometimes split personalities.
Shadow images reveal our evil.
They can also show us our potential.
These figures are mysterious strangers who,
like Jesus in his ministry,
are 'signs of contradiction'.

The American western is one of the most popular genres that uses the device of the mysterious stranger. He seems to come out of nowhere at the beginning of the film, riding into a town, gaining the support of the good, alienating the bad, called on to administer or vindicate justice, especially in conquering the villain. Then almost as mysteriously, he rides out of town. George Stevens' 1953 classic **Shane** is one of the best and best-known of the 'stranger' westerns, with Alan Ladd in the title role of the mysterious hero.

The stranger is a sign of contradiction. This is a phrase used of Jesus himself in Luke's Gospel. The aged prophet Simeon tells Mary and Joseph that their son is destined for the rise and fall of many in Israel. He is to be a sign of contradiction. The beginning of his ministry, as related in the Gospels, has him appearing at the River Jordan to be baptised.

When he begins to preach the good news of the kingdom and of repentance, it is evident that he is a sign of contradiction. The good, the people, hurry to him for healing, for consolation and for teaching that has authority. The bad, the religious leaders of the day with double standards, resent him, try all kinds of devices to trick and trap him. Some of them plot his death. Some know that he comes from Nazareth, and they are not necessarily impressed. Nathaniel asks what good can come out of Nazareth. It is as if Jesus came from almost nowhere.

In John's Gospel there are reports that some know that he is a prophet and from Galilee. Others heard that he came from Bethlehem. Crowds follow him eagerly but when the teaching is too hard, they walk away.

Crowds hail his entry into Jerusalem. The same crowds scream for his death only days later. For so many, Jesus was a stranger. He came into the lives of his people. He challenged and changed. He was a mysterious stranger.

We are often mysterious strangers to ourselves. At times we feel we are in control. At other times we are caught off guard; we think, feel, behave in ways that surprise or shock us.

There have been many stories of split personality. The most popular has been Robert Louis Stevenson's **Dr. Jekyll and Mr. Hyde.** Written in the Victorian era, an age of external respectability which covered a great deal of evil and bizarre behaviour, the story is of a man with faith in science and human endeavour who usurps the role of super-human control and unleashes his dark side, a shadow inner self. The evil Mr. Hyde is the respected Dr. Jekyll.

There have been many versions of this story. It is a point of reference for others. A powerful film on the religious cults of the '70s and '80s used footage from the Spencer Tracy version of **Dr. Jekyll and Mr. Hyde** and highlighted the light and dark in society, cult victim, cult leader and cult foe, the debriefer. The film was significantly titled **Split Image.**

The shadow side of self reveals aspects of personality that we might not readily acknowledge. The shadow is certainly a mysterious stranger. The shadow side of self can also make us aware of undeveloped potential, a side of us which has a greater power for good. It is said that this shadow side of self can reveal to us the growing edge of our experience. It can be the way for God to challenge us.

While 'grace builds on nature' and our 'selves' must be affirmed, the asceticism so necessary for human and for spiritual growth comes from being challenged where we have least hold or control.

Symbolic figures like Dr. Jekyll and Mr. Hyde are necessary to mirror (larger than life) our shadow selves. We will not necessarily like to look — but we need to look. This means that shadow and mysterious stranger-figures have the potential for salvation. In an offbeat way, they are Christ-figures.

The most striking of the good/evil mysterious strangers is Clint Eastwood in **High Plains Drifter.** He comes out of the haze. At the end of the film he returns into the haze. In the meantime, he appears in a typical western town as an itinerant gunfighter. The 'poor' of the town are attracted to him — widows, the lame, the oppressed. The powerful, the wealthy, the brutally strong are hostile. He gathers up his followers, urging them to leave the town — a remnant to be saved.

One night he paints the town red, places a signpost at the edge of the lake beside which the town stands. The sign reads 'Hell'. He then sets the town alight and stands in the midst of the plains wielding his whip. It is obvious that a whip-lashing avenger in 'Hell' must be a demon. Yet this stranger has rescued and saved the poor.

Clint Eastwood's stranger is a variation on the Jekyll-Hyde character. A more straightforward earlier western that resembles it is **No Name on the Bullet** starring Audie Murphy.

Films considered oddities in their day had more obviously kindly strangers, almost angels. Ian Hunter was a mysterious prisoner in Frank Borzage's **Strange Cargo** (1941) and transformed the lives of tough Clark Gable and Joan Crawford. The black and white photography sometimes suggested a Christ-like aura.

In one of the many tough police thrillers of the '50s, **City That Never**

Sleeps, Chill Wills seems to personify the city of Chicago in his opening voice-over commentary and then appears as Gig Young's partner on the beat, saving him from ruining his life and career. Sidney Poitier, so often portraying characters who do good, came to a small town to change people's lives as **Brother John.**

Two films have enigmatic strangers whose behaviour seems more demonic than angelic, yet their effect on a family's life seems to be transforming and for the better: Terence Stamp in Pasolini's **Teorema** and Sting, who does seem to be a devil in **Brimstone and Treacle** (from a screenplay by Dennis Potter). They might be seen as antichrists. But they belong to the small but important gallery of shadow stranger-figures. ■

GANDHI . . . *Richard Attenborough directs Ben Kingsley in the Oscar-winning portrait of and tribute to the non-violent Mahatma.*

28

Universal Christ-figures

*The study of world religions
shows the deep longing
of the heart for meaning.
The Christian story is parallelled
in the history and literature
of these religions.*

It seems rather presumptuous, perhaps offensive to some who do not share the Christian faith in Jesus, to call important figures from world religions, Christ-figures.

Some years ago a phrase was current in theology, 'anonymous Christians'. It was intended as a favourable term to indicate that any person who was committed religiously was saved. Since, in Christian belief, faith and salvation come through Jesus, the religious person who does not know him could be seen as an 'anonymous Christian'. This was a step better than referring to all peoples of faith as non-Christians. It is realised now in many spheres how inadequate (and arrogant or insulting) it is to define a group merely by negatives.

Catholic thought since the '60s has tried to grapple with the reality of many religions, especially the major world religions of Judaism, Hinduism, Buddhism, Islam. While the Old Testament spoke of a 'chosen people', it was always in the context of God's love for all peoples — not an exclusive favouritism. The thrust of the New Testament is that God wishes all to be saved and come to the knowledge of the truth. While Christians see Jesus as the mediator between God and humankind, God's gracing presence in our world has not been confined to the Judaeo-Christian tradition and communities.

The study of religions shows that there is a deep desire in the hearts of all men and women for meaning, even for a divine reality, a God. The myths of major religions, of local worship, of isolated peoples, of peoples of every century, dramatise these yearnings. Patterns of religious stories occur; the same elements emerge. There are myriad stories of human sinfulness, disaster, repentance and redemption, of divine beings coming among human beings, of wonders, of heroism, self-sacrifice and glorification.

While Jesus' story has a unique style in its telling, the climax of Old Testament spirituality and the beauty and wisdom of the person of Jesus, it nevertheless is part of the pattern of religious storytelling, myth-making.

It is in this sense that we can validly, not presumptuously, speak about figures from world religious cultures in the context of Christ-figures.

An excellent example from history and from the screen is Mahatma Gandhi. A more conventional action-study was the 1960s' **Nine Hours to Rama.** But Richard Attenborough's Oscar-winning portrait of the Mahatma, **Gandhi,** a film principally for western audiences but acceptable also to Indian audiences, showed a great 20th century figure and his growth from a dapper English-trained lawyer in 1890s' South Africa to a community leader able to endure violence and prison and to speak of courage, to a national hero and spiritual leader.

Ultimately, as a world-figure with his creed of non-violence and his martyr's death, he has become a figure whose ideals have the power to inspire decades after his death.

John Briley's screenplay shows Gandhi as a man of Hindu religious traditions and practice. It highlights his awareness of God, his God-language, prayer, speaking of God's presence and his law, his respect for religion and use of traditional signs. It offers his explanation of his religious training in a sequence with the American journalist by the sea. Gandhi sang the hymns about non-violence as a boy but had not understood them. He had a respect for the Hindu tradition — but fought against the caste-system, saw the lack of harmony between Muslim and Hindu in India, saw the Muslims as a minority with consequent tensions and political fears, with the eruption of violence and civil war.

A climax of the film was Gandhi's appeal, during his fast, for Hindus and Muslims to lay down arms — he then asked a repentant Hindu who said he was in hell to adopt and train a Muslim child in atonement for his own violence. Gandhi, while a Hindu, spoke of his own experience as being trained in reading from both Hindu scriptures and the Koran. Gandhi, therefore, was a figure for all religions. At the end of the film he declared that he was Hindu, Muslim, Sikh, Christian.

The Christian focus is dramatised in his encounter with clergyman Charlie Andrews, as he walked down the South African street risking physical attack, ready to turn the other cheek. He reminded Charlie Andrews that these were the words of Jesus himself. Gandhi's perception was that Jesus meant what he said and he realised that this would be provocative. Muslim, Hindu and Christian tradition combined to create a philosophy of non-violence, non-cooperation. Vivid sequences in the film: Indian protesters lying down before cavalry in South Africa, the Salt March to the sea, the rank on rank of Indians approaching a mine and being bashed by soldiers' rifle butts, all highlight this.

Since Gandhi himself chose to use Christian language about himself, he can be appropriately called a Christ-figure.

Jesus was a Jewish figure. His spirituality was that of the Old Testament. Jesus, therefore, resembles Jewish figures in literature and film with their cultural and spiritual heritage. Parallels should not be stretched but the Jew has been the martyr of all ages, often the Christians' victim. Useful cinema examples are versions of Bernard Malamud's **The Fixer** and Isaac Bashevis Singer's **The Magician of Lublin.**

The Fixer probes the most basic human values of existence, suffering and fidelity to oneself and conscience. Jakob Bok, the fixer, played by Alan Bates, is the Jew, the martyr of all time and of our century: the man who appeals to humanity's sense of justice and readily evokes audience horror at man's inhumanity to man. A martyr suffers extremely; he also suffers unjustly. This film relentlessly moves the audience with a massing of scenes of cruelty and, especially, of frustration. A martyr witnesses to beliefs. Bok clings to his innocence against all odds, including a release from prison in an amnesty. He refuses, preferring to become an international test-case for anti-semitism. He becomes a hero, but not before degradation when only the repeated muttering of 'I am a man' keeps him sane and capable of continuing.

The film shows someone finding his dignity through suffering. Not believing in God, Bok goes through his passion and achieves an earthly resurrection. The film believes in the religious nature of suffering and it places its hope in vindication. The parallels with Job are obvious. The resemblances to Jesus are also obvious.

The worldly magician of Lublin eventually becomes a recluse, a holy man to whom pilgrims come, a saint.

The two holy men of the other major world religions have been the subject of films. The story of the Buddha has been seen in the version of Herman Hesse's **Siddhartha.** Anthony Quinn starred in an epic treatment of the life and mission of Muhammad, **Muhammad, the Messenger of God.** Muslim tradition does not permit the images of the prophet, so the subjective eye of the camera was that of the prophet. ∎

29

The Australian Context

Australia is not a religious society.
Material success is a goal
but dark irony is a prevalent tone.
The Land offers meaning
and there is a need
for old and new myth-making.

The apostle Paul frequently exhorted fellow-Christians to be imitators of him as he was of Christ. He presented himself in his letters as a Christ-figure. And the invitation was to men and women of all cultures. In fact, Paul stressed how the good news of Jesus was for all and that he adapted his own life-style to be a Christ-figure for all: . . . 'made myself the slave of everyone to win as many as I could . . . a Jew to the Jews . . . free of the law to win those who have no Law . . . I made myself all things to all men in order to save some at any cost' (1Cor. 9:19-23).

It is relevant to look at (or look for) Christ-figures in the Australian context.

One of the difficulties in considering matters religious in Australian history and society is that Australia is considered to be the first secular society. Western culture in the 18th century was on the verge of the Industrial Revolution as well as political and social revolutions and upheaval. The French Revolution took place in the second year of European settlement of Australia. By this time, Christianity had lost much of its official status in European nations.

The 18th century has been called the Age of Reason, of Enlightenment. It was not an Age of Faith. One would not immediately expect to find obvious Christ-figures in our literature and art.

Manning Clark, in his imaginative writing of Australian history, suggests that there were three representative groups under the gum trees at Sydney Cove on 26th January, 1788. There were the men of the Enlightenment, Governor Philip, officials and marines; there were members of the established Church of England amongst officials, marines and convicts; there were Catholics among the convicts, Catholics who could also represent the range of non-established, non-conformist Christian denominations. The bewildered Aborigines looked on.

19th century Australia was a secular society begun in oppression and a convict spirit that was anti-authoritarian. The century of opening up of the land, settlement, exploration, gold rushes and the building of communication links meant a pioneering spirit and a capacity for surviving hardship. Then there were the hostilities, the benevolence, the paternalism towards the Aborigines. A goal of 19th century Australia was success, symbolised perhaps by commonwealth federation in 1901.

It has been pointed out that this pattern of moving from hardship in country of origin, poor migrants working desperately for material success and moving up the social scale, has been the materialistic success pattern for each group: convict, Irish, post-war Europeans and, in the '80s, Asian migrants and refugees. The focus in Australia has been on this world.

Despite this there has been an ironic undertone to the Australian outlook and humour. Faced with tyrannies of distance, of seasons, destruction, there has been a bleak horizon and pessimistic touch: 'Such Is Life'. Bleakness came to some heroism and meaning at Gallipoli and on the Kokoda Trail. However, many creative spirits have not been able to grow up in this environment and there has always been the phenomenon of the expatriates: poets, novelists, painters, musicians, actors. Theatre director Michael Blakemore has made a cinema memoir highlighting these clashes in **A Personal History of the Australian Surf. Confessions of a Straight Poofter,** a title which insinuates a great deal about traditional Australian attitudes.

However, the land itself has come back into focus as a way of understanding life in Australia. We are more and more getting in touch with 'The Land's Meaning'. Poet A. D. Hope in his satirical '40s poem 'Australia' concluded with the wish that prophets, as in Old Testament times, might again come from the desert. Judith Wright in 'Bullocky' (also 1940s) speaks of the Promised Land, fruitful over the Moses-like pioneers buried in it.

The poets have led us to Old Testament figures. Perhaps the Aboriginal myths of Dreamtime, heroes and the sacred, will lead us further into the Land's Meaning.

The last two hundred years have been centuries of suffering both for black and for white. This suffering needs to be redeemed. We are not short of martyrs in history and art: the Aboriginals massacred, portrayed in many documentaries: **Women of the Sun, A Shifting Dreaming, Two Laws, Lousy Little Sixpence.** Convict-victims like Rufus Dawes in Marcus Clark's **For the Term of His Natural Life,** convicts-turned-bushranger like **Mad Dog Morgan** and executed-bushrangers-become-folk-heroes like Ned Kelly, are part of the heritage. The suffering needs continued interpretation.

If Australia is seen to be a promised land, then significant saviour-figures seem to emerge. On the screens of the early '80s, the two significant heroes are **The Man from Snowy River** and **Phar Lap.** They emphasise the battler who succeeds.

Breakthrough figures include feminists like Sybilla in **My Brilliant Career** and Laura in **The Getting of Wisdom.**

In looking from Australia to Asia, there are the Australians caught up in the Philippines in **Far East** or in Indonesia in **The Year of Living Dangerously.**

While Breaker Morant declared himself to be a pagan before going to his execution and his fellow pagan, Peter Handcock, could write at the end of his last letter to his wife, 'Australia Forever! Amen', the two young men of **Gallipoli** prepared to go to war and to die — and the golden-haired idealist Archie does die while the larrikin-hero Frank lives — are, at least, symbolic figures of selfless giving. It is interesting to note that in an age of recognisable pop-saviours on the screen, the Australian cinema's leader-figure — sufferer in a mindlessly violent society and rescuer of the victims and leader to safety in Paradise — is **Mad Max.**

From a young secular society, perhaps it is not so surprising that the most popular saviour-figure should be a blend of comic strip and myth-making. ■

THE STRANGLER OF RILLINGTON PLACE . . . *Antichrists can be spectacular or mundane. Richard Attenborough as mass murderer Reginald Christie.*

30

Antichrist Figures

The Christ-figure resembles Jesus significantly.
Characteristics of Jesus himself
are thereby highlighted.
Embodiments of evil
have appeared in every culture.
In the Christian tradition,
embodiments of evil, antichrists,
have parallelled and parodied
the Jesus-characteristics.

The Judaeo-Christian tradition is filled with the revelation of a God who intervenes and acts creatively and graciously in our world. Since all the world and all peoples are his (Exodus 19), he can love and be with specially chosen and consecrated groups and individuals. Over the centuries of the Old Testament period, the qualities of God were spoken of in metaphor, gradually personified (Breath, Word, Spirit, Wisdom) so that when 'the fullness of time' came, there was a mentality and language to comprehend and describe the presence of Jesus, the Son of the Father, in this human world. Jesus was godliness and goodness incarnate.

By the end of the Old Testament era, it was not difficult for the Jews to imagine the embodiments of evil. Although they had no pictures or statues of their God, they had used many visual images in their religious poetry and in the prophetic oracles. Yahweh as the true Shepherd King was one of the most vivid. But, as the religious movements of the East influenced Jewish thinking, an 'apocalyptic' mentality, with its relative symbolism, exotic use of numbers, colours and larger-than-life personalities, pervaded the Old Testament.

'Apocalyptic' refers to special (eventually spectacular) revelations. The shift of interest and theological emphasis was from this present world and the ordinary way of living to a transformation of this world. Whether our earth was to become different or it was to pass away, even be destroyed by fire, the focus was on 'the last times', the 'end of our time', and the beginning of either a new earth, a new kingdom or a heavenly existence. The theological emphasis on the last things: death, judgement, heaven, hell, is called 'eschatalogical'.

But eastern religion also pitted good against evil, symbolising the final times as a battle between the forces of light and the forces of darkness. It was as if good and evil were equal, coming from two distinct and opposing sources. This is called 'Dualism'. Traces of this imagery can be found in the prophet Ezekiel (chapter 39-40) with the giant figure of Gog of Magog.

The New Testament Book of Revelation is the most significant of the apocalyptic books and the struggle of good and evil is powerfully described.

However, with its faith in the saving death and resurrection of Jesus, the Book of Revelation is not dualistic. God is sole creator and Father and takes the redeemed to the 'new and heavenly Jerusalem'. This is the language also of the Gospels.

However, dualist traditions continued into the Christian era and surfaced in strange sects with bizarre behaviour, overstressing the difference between spiritual perfection and corruption of the flesh, often falling victim to the latter.

St. Augustine, who was for some time a Manichean (who subscribed to dualist theories) is blamed for a subconscious dualism in Christian theology, especially that of morality. This confrontation between symbols of good and symbols of evil has pervaded Christianity.

The Old Testament book of Daniel (167-164 BC) offers a vivid picture of God himself. In chapter 7, in visionary language, he is described as the Ancient of Days, old, white-haired, attended by a court of thousands. In the book of Daniel, God's messengers are described, especially Michael the warrior (12:1). One of the New Testament missions of Michael is to confront, do battle with and conquer evil in the dragon-Satan.

> 'The great dragon, the primeval serpent, known as the Devil or Satan, who had deceived all the world, was hurled down to the earth and his angels were hurled down with him.' (Revelation 12:7ff, esp. v 9.)

Chapter 13 describes monstrous apocalyptic beasts. We now have in Scripture anti-God figures, devils.

This symbolic incarnation of evil is taken for granted in the Gospels. All kinds of evil spirits inhabit ordinary human beings. Jesus casts out many of them. Judas, Jesus' betrayer, is associated with this evil. Satan enters into him. He is in the power of the Prince of Darkness. He goes out from the Last Supper — and it is night (John 13). In the Garden of Gethsemane Jesus is greeted by Judas as a friend and he betrays Jesus with a sign of intimacy, embrace and kiss (John 18). The Gospels tell us of Judas' remorse. The Acts tell us of the culmination of evil in despair and suicide (Acts 1).

Almost immediately, the first disciples of Jesus experienced hostility from individuals and forces against Christ. These forces were considered deceivers, tricksters, wolves in sheep's clothing.

Gospel sayings of Jesus echo these experiences, associating them with eschatalogical teaching as well as dire and awesome apocalyptic imagery. Key texts are Matthew 24:23-25, 2 Thess. 2:3-4,9 (Paul's vivid description of antichrists), 2 Peter 2:1-3, 1 John 4:1 (John's firm description of the spirit of the antichrist), 2 John 7-11, Revelation 13. The Devil, the Evil One, was associated with these deceivers, false prophets. The oracles and visions from the book of Revelation, however, were soon to be taken out of context and misapplied to individuals and religious movements.

Over the centuries, preachers have offered contemporary interpretations of these mysterious prophecies and warnings. At the end of the first Christian millenium, sects abounded anticipating the Second Coming. Religious sects of the 19th and 20th centuries (aided by advertising campaigns and mass media) have heralded the coming of Jesus or of his representatives, cult and sect figures. The 20th century has seen the Nazis proclaim the thousand-year Reich and Christians see East-West superpower struggles as 'apocalypse now'.

Over the centuries myths and legends, like that of Dracula or of werewolves have grown up. Witchcraft and superstition and their inquisitorial repression have left the world a heritage of antichrist figures and rituals. Mediaeval art, gargoyles, Last Judgment paintings (borrowing heavily from images of the book of Revelation) illustrate fearful belief in the power of the Devil and the incarnation of evil. The Church has always had rituals of exorcism. The '60s 'God is dead' upheaval in western society gave rise to a new phase of interest in the occult and astrology, in mass-appeal novels and horror-films.

Just as the Christ-figure resembles Jesus Christ in significant ways so that the Jesus-characteristics give meaning to the figure as well as illuminate the perceptions of Jesus himself, so the antichrist figures derive their meaning from Jesus. They resemble him significantly by parallels, by contrast, by parody and mockery of his personality, his life and its Gospel proclamation — false messiahs, false prophets have appeared, performing great signs and wonders for the purpose of deceiving God's people. ■

THE BROTHERHOOD OF SATAN . . . *What would a devil incarnate look like? Damien in* The Omen *series or* Rosemary's Baby *or . . . your average folks in this satanic tale?*

31

Incarnations of Evil

If Jesus is a divine and human person,
then it is not unthinkable or unimaginable
to have a diabolical and human person.
While traditionally there have been
devil-incarnate legends,
contemporary horror and realism
have made this antichrist more credible.

The mystery of the Incarnation is that the Word of God became 'flesh' and, in a particular time and in a particular place, 'dwelt amongst us'. Jesus of Nazareth revealed himself as Son of the Father, 'Abba'. He is also the son of Mary. Like us humans in all things, with the exception of sin, sinfulness (evil turning away from the Father), he shows that the divine and human can be one. From the imaginative perspective, let alone a theological perspective, this means that 'lesser spiritual beings' can also be incarnate; that angels and devils and Satan, or his 'offspring' can dwell amongst us.

Whether this is the mind of the Old and New Testament writers is one thing — and unimportant because of the presence of Jesus who 'conquered sin and death'. But for the offbeat Christian tradition, for the legends and occult myths developed in Dark Ages and mediaeval times and lingering through the centuries, demonic incarnations hold fascinating sway. Sacrilegious images and rituals, pseudo-religious and irreligious, lure the curious, the insecure and the bitter. And what better way to portray these antichrist figures than by parallels and comparisons with the Gospel accounts of Jesus?

If God can live on Earth, why can't the Devil?

Many of the Devil-on-Earth stories are a more sophisticated or obvious version of fairy stories or nightmares. They are metaphors of evil, of shadow facets of the human psyche. Authors, screen-writers and film-makers are attracted by the creative potential of the plots and characters and use, often most effectively, the rituals and trappings of religion, the vocabulary of piety and theology. But the aim is suspense and shock, the staple ingredients of the horror film. This is not to deny imaginative insight via these metaphors. But the stories and films are, for the most part, appreciated (or derided) as horror-fantasy and not as 'realistic'.

Hollywood's Universal Studios in the '30s and '40s produced classics of this kind, beginning with **Dracula** and **Frankenstein.** Hammer Studios had Peter Cushing and Christopher Lee reviving these stories with colour and special effects, British style, from the '50s to the '70s. Storytellers like novelist Dennis Wheatley supplied plots and titles. Nastassia Kinski, long before **Tess** and a star career, appeared with Lee and Richard Widmark in **To The Devil A Daughter** (1975).

European directors, steeped in Christian tradition (Catholic and reformed), have sometimes taken a more serious, less box-office approach to incarnations of the Devil. Scandinavian director Carl-Theodor Dreyer, with a Lutheran background, made many religious films ranging from **Vampyr** to **The Passion of Joan of Arc.**

A silent film, **Leaves from Satan's Book,** used fable and religious allegory to portray the presence of Satan on Earth. Episodes included a Judas story, a Renaissance story where the Devil, incarnated as the Grand Inquisitor, allows a friar to be tempted sensually and fall, a French Revolution story and a 1918 Finnish story with Satan as a Rasputin-like monk.

Marcel Carne in 1942 used a mediaeval setting for **Les Visiteurs du Soir (Visitors of the Night)** where the intentions are of diabolical corruption but appearances are elegant. Ingmar Bergman, again with a Lutheran reformed background, has serious mediaeval pageants, **The Seventh Seal** and **The Virgin Spring,** as well as a comedy-of-manners parody, **The Devil's Eye.** The Europeans ask for more thoughtful response to their allegories of good and evil.

However, the film that brought incarnations of evil into prominence (both critically and commercially) was Roman Polanski's vivid and absorbing version of Ira Levin's **Rosemary's Baby** (1968). An important factor in its influence was its contemporary setting, its realistic style and its acknowledgement of eccentric members of covens and their dabbling in satanism and witchcraft. Seances, held seriously or 'for fun', are common enough. **Rosemary's Baby** was taken more seriously, emotionally if not intellectually, than costume horror films.

1968 was also a period of critique, reaction and reassessment of religious belief and practice. In theological study, it was the period of the 'God-is-dead' theology, though many theologians wanted a moratorium on the word 'God' in order to re-evaluate the transcendent. The '70s' interest in the apocalyptic and the superstitious has enabled **Rosemary's Baby** to remain an influential and disturbing film.

The screenplay offers a Catholic (lapsed) couple (Mia Farrow and John Cassavetes) and the context of a New York visit by Pope Paul VI to the United Nations (glimpsed on TV news). Rosemary's husband sells his soul to the Devil through the coven's officials for a successful stage career. In so doing he becomes an evil foster-father — and John Cassavetes has an ability to appear demonic.

In his union with his wife (and Polanksi uses dream techniques atmospherically), she is 'overshadowed' by Satan. There are signs and portents (associated with witchcraft) linked with her pregnancy, and her friends (led by a smilingly sinister Ruth Gordon) are like mock-Gospel figures and disciples. Rosemary gives birth to her son, experiencing a weirdness in giving birth — but, as the baby lies (unseen by the audience) in its requiem-black crib, Rosemary's maternal instincts overcome her revulsion. Satan is incarnate.

Hollywood offered a sequel in 1976, **Look What's Happened to Rosemary's Baby,** re-presenting some of the same themes, showing the man who is devilish — and who is in danger of being redeemed. However, the treatment was television-audience oriented and made little impact.

But the 'incarnation' films that continued the impact were **The Omen** series. Based on the Book of Revelation references, especially to the number of the Beast as 666, a diabolical child is substituted in a Rome hospital (born June 6, 1966) to the wife of the U.S. Ambassador to Britain (Lee Remick and Gregory Peck).

The Omen is visually violent and Damien, the boy, is clearly demonic. Born to power, he is educated under William Holden's care in the U.S. in the sequel, **Damien — Omen II.** He is obviously on the path to world power.

In **The Final Conflict,** played by handsome Sam Neill, he has wealth and power and wields them cruelly. The series goes biblical with a Jesus-figure (unfortunately kitschy) at the end with the triumph of good.

In the contemporary imagination, via these cinema images, the incarnation of the Devil is possible. ■

THE EXORCIST . . . *Linda Blair was possessed. Ellen Burstyn was her distraught mother. Max Von Sydow was the exorcist.*

32

Demonic Possession

Theology has a language of God's grace
that describes his dwelling in us
and the indwelling of the Spirit.
There is also a tradition of evil spirits
inhabiting human beings, possessing them,
and of their being cast out by exorcism.

In Old Testament language, the Spirit of God could seize a prophet and empower him to perform symbolic actions to indicate God's will. In New Testament language, Paul speaks of himself as a Christ-figure: 'I live, no longer I, but Christ lives in me' (Gal.2:19). John's Gospel, especially in the Last Discourse, uses images like that of the vine and branches to highlight the unity of his disciples with him, the union of the Father and himself. ('Father, may they be one in us, as you are in me and I am in you ... that they may be one as we are one. With me in them and you in me, may they be so completely one ...' John 17:21-23).

The language of the theology of grace is that of the 'in-dwelling' of God, especially that of the Spirit.

As with incarnation, there can be comparisons and parallels with demonic indwelling. Satan is described as entering the heart of Judas Iscariot (John 13:2). In fact, this indwelling of evil spirits is a dominant feature of the Gospels. All kinds of spirits, devilish as well as tormenting spirits of depression and ill health, inhabit human beings. Jesus casts them out, from one to 'Legion'. The casting out of these devils becomes, at times, a theological discussion point and a sign of the authenticity of his mission.

The Good News shows some fascination with the inhabiting spirits and phenomena associated with their presence. It is, therefore, not surprising if possession and exorcism have been constantly in the Christian consciousness.

From earliest times the Church has had prayers and rituals for exorcisms. During the Middle Ages, witchcraft and diabolical possession were a commonplace theme. Manuscripts, gargoyles on Cathedrals, symbolic tokens remind us of the ugliness and horror of such presence of evil. The Inquisition and its trials continued and exploited this atmosphere.

Many saints have been associated with diabolical assaults, like the Curé of Ars, John Vianney, in 19th century France. Stories from the Church's missionary activity, of Marie-Therese Noblet in Papua New Guinea, for example, inspire and/or alarm. It is not surprising that films, especially from the '70s, have taken up possessed anti-christ figures and exorcisms.

The story of the Ursulines of Loudon in the time of Cardinal Richelieu has been novelised by Aldous Huxley, dramatised by John Whiting and brought to the screen, in Poland with **Mother Joan of the Angels,** and in England with Ken Russell's **The Devils.** While the nuns, women enclosed unwillingly in a convent because they had no prospects or dowry, were not possessed by evil spirits, their hysteria (frustration and repressed sexuality) was fanned for political purposes and gave every sign of diabolical frenzy, physical contortions, symptoms of fits and blasphemous behaviour.

Ken Russell, never a reticent director, has visualised religious madness and evil at the service of intellectual strategies and coldly-burning ambition. This evil control is far more insidious and demonic than the 'possession' it exploits.

But the film that made impact with a contemporary possession story was, of course, **The Exorcist.** Author William Peter Blatty had investigated an alleged possession case in Georgetown in the '40s. He used his Jesuit education and Jesuit advisers (as did the film) to ensure some 'authenticity'.

In the film, the Devil enters a child, an innocent victim, and controls her life, turning her into a blasphemous monster, a destroyer and an incarnation of antichrist hatred. Famous special effects (facial corruption, head-turns, letters appearing on a stomach) gave the film a notoriety that sometimes distracted from the meaning of the film.

While non-Christian audiences could take it as a contemporary horror story with as little religious impact as a Dracula shocker, Christians and Catholics (especially those who had 'lapsed') often found the film far more alarming.

Acerbic New York critic Pauline Kael suggested that it was the biggest pro-Catholic screen poster since **The Bells of St. Mary's.** Her point was that under the '70s cinema style was an age-old story (we remember Job) of human beings, without fault of their own, being assaulted by a spiritual power that they could not dominate and seemingly abandoned by God. The Evil One, without warning and without reason, entered and took possession.

Linda Blair's Regan, the possessed girl, suffered. But her suffering had dire repercussions. It seemed to criticise the worldly United States way of life, the loss of values, the superficial world of moviedom. Regan's mother was rendered helpless and distraught. Associates died and the priest sent to exorcise the Devil suffered crises of faith and physical abuse. Max von Sydow as the exorcist sustained the powerfully melodramatic sequences of the struggle between Satan and the power of God through the Church.

The Exorcist, well-made by William Friedkin and well-acted, is the strongest cinema example of possession.

The sequel, **Exorcist II — The Heretic,** was not well-received. Richard Burton played a priest confronting the Devil in Regan, once again a victim. The screenplay veered between interest in psychological therapy and in an anthropological view of tribal religions and myths. Perhaps it shifted emphasis too radically for audiences to sustain interest from the original.

One of the unfortunate results of a film being a success is that there are many derivative sequels and exploitative spin-offs. This was definitely the case with **The Exorcist.** By the time movie-makers tried to outdo the macabre special effects and invent outlandish plot situations on which to hang the effects, possession had become just another trend and, in fact, a bit of a horror giggle.

Two derivative films which attempted a more serious approach were a Negro-parallel, **Abby,** and an Italian-set story called, significantly, **The Antichrist.**

However, the Italians, as they have done with westerns, gangster and horror films, take a trend and give it the wide-screen spectacular exploitative treatment. As with the 'spaghetti westerns' there were many 'spaghetti occult' films with titles like **House of Exorcism, Behind the Door.** They ran their course with mock-hilarity and scare tactics.

But the frightening implications of **The Exorcist** still remain. ■

THE DAY AFTER . . . *Is a nuclear blast a sign of the gate to hell? This American telemovie shocked and frightened audiences when it was released in 1983.*

33

Gates-of-Hell Symbolism

The old vision of the heavens,
the earth and the underworld
was used in Scripture
for images of heaven and hell.
Evil power was associated
with the 'Gates of Hell'.
Occult thrillers have used this symbol
with some enthusiasm.

It is surprising that for the Old Testament people, belief in a life after death came so late in their history, about 200 BC. Even then it was not universally accepted. The wealthy and traditionalist faction of Jesus' day, the Sadducees, did not share this belief. In fact, they mocked Jesus with attempts at ridiculous hypotheses about a woman with seven brothers as her successive husbands and the problem of whose wife she would be in 'heaven'.

However, the Hebrews' neighbours in Assyria and Egypt had long believed in a life beyond death. The pyramids are a lasting monument to this. Stories of journeys, descriptions of places, a variety of deities were part of belief in life after death.

By the time the Jews developed their language and theology, it was the period of apocalyptic imagination, vivid imagery, esoteric and symbolic use of numbers, colours, names and a hierarchy of beings between the deity and humans: good and evil beings, angels and devils. They were associated with the language of heaven and hell — heaven above, hell below.

The New Testament reflects this language and symbolism. In the famous Petrine text of Matthew 16, where Jesus promises Peter the keys of the kingdom of heaven, part of the promise is that 'the gates of the underworld can never hold out' against the Church. Commentators note that the personified 'gates' suggest the powers of evil that tempt us and then imprison mankind in eternal death.

This 'underworld' is mentioned in the ancient hymn Paul quotes to the Philippians, reflecting the understanding of the threefold division of creation, 'in the heavens, on earth and in the underworld' (Phil.2:10). John's Revelation also refers to it (Rev.5:3,13).

Christian tradition and I Pet.3:18-22 speak of Jesus saving those who had died in the Old Testament era and who were waiting for their salvation. This was called Jesus' 'descent into hell', into the lower regions, under the earth. The first century Christians, with the powerful apocalyptic imagery exciting them, developed a vision of the experienced loss of God as hell, a place of fire, of eternal worms gnawing, of sorrow and gnashing of teeth.

The symbolic beasts of the Books of Daniel and of Revelation were associated with devils, and hell was a place of eternal and monstrous suffering.

The long tradition blending themes from Scripture, popular imagination, superstition and visual art produced stories of damnation, diabolical struggles and torment. An over-literal interpretation of Scripture, as with incarnations and possessions, has meant that stories of entrances to hell have appealed to storytellers and film-makers. In the '70s and '80s, screenwriters were able to locate such 'gates of hell' even in the centre of a modern city.

A flashy, star-studded example of this kind of story is **The Sentinel** which combines Italian priests and rituals, verses from Milton's 'Paradise Lost' on hell with a New York apartment building, murders and police investigations. The apartment is the gate of hell. Here a lonely sentinel (priest or nun) sits out a term of guardianship. Candidature for this post is attempted suicide. Christina Raines, a fashion model, is the beleaguered heroine who escapes from an horrendous collection of ghouls raised up from hell to pursue her, only to become the next sentinel. It is all nonsense — but dressed up both solemnly and sensationally as the truth about hell.

More popular was the series of films on a diabolically possessed house at Amityville. **The Amityville Horror** purported to be 'true' and the promotion campaign was strong on persuading potential patrons that this was another of those authenticated mysterious stories. An ordinary family buys a home (photographed often at night, its facade resembling a face) but it terrorises them, destroys their parish priest. In the basement they discover links with the celebrated history of New England witchcraft in the 17th century. Beneath this is the fiery opening to hell.

The popularity of the film brought a follow-up, a 'sequel', **Amityville: The Possession,** where we see the demons of the house possess and destroy another family — but the audience knows how the evil spirits got through. Then came **Amityville — 3D,** an enjoyably scary exercise in horror devices with science coming to the rescue where religion has failed. But the monsters also destroy the scientists.

This wearing out of a theme by commercial exploitation indicates that whatever the serious approach to the original story, the material is quite sensational rather than factual. Superstition can self-destruct by over-kill. In fact, the box office-busting **Ghostbusters** played for laughs, exaggerations of this kind of gate-of-hell material.

Some suggest that, while the 'gate of hell' story is popular apocalyptic imagination, the settings of these stories suggest something more serious, a critique or condemnation of aspects of this society's lifestyle.

The Devil's Rain opens with Hieronymus Bosch paintings and moves to the modern American West inhabited by satanists from the 17th century with their legacy of puritanical witch-hunting and burning, seeking to possess souls and trap them in rain controlled by the Devil. The film portrays the black side of obsessive American self-righteousness.

In **Children of the Corn,** a Stephen King short story, children destroy the adults and try to make their town religious — a moral majority can be cruel in its manipulation and control. **Deadly Blessing** is set in one of those mid-western religious communities that lives in the past, quaintly-spoken, standing against machinery and things modern, all in the name of God and the Bible. But it is a hotbed of suppressed evil and rebellion. In fact, a diabolical incubus rises out of the ground, a house opens up and drags characters down into hell. Such a community is a gate of hell.

While the trappings of Scripture are associated with contemporary superstition, the gate of hell, even in occult thrillers, can serve as a useful symbol of evil. ■

THE REVENGE OF FRANKENSTEIN . . . *Nature fights back as*
The Birds or Jaws or the Frankenstein monster.

34

Malevolent Nature Symbols

God created a good world.
But plague, devastation and
the continued menace of accident
as well as preying animals
have always offered stories of disaster
and of monster embodiments of evil.

Jesus told his followers to consider the birds of the air and the lilies of the field to understand God's abundant love and providence for humankind. On a stronger note, thunder, clouds and lightning have accompanied the special Old Testament appearances of God, theophanies. Nature, the world, is a created wonder. 'God saw all that he had made and it was very good'. (Gn.2).

But just as there is sin in the human heart and evil spirits can possess human beings both guilty and innocent, so nature is associated with or used by anti-God forces. The majestic, over-awing power of some manifestations of nature terrifies (and has always terrified) us and we have seen the presence of destructive malice in nature. In Walt Disney's **Fantasia,** the Devil himself materialised, plucking men and women from this world, to the music of Mussorgsky's 'Night on Bald Mountain'.

Living in this world has always been precarious: natural disasters, fierce animals and venomous reptiles, pretty poisonous flowers and plants. Human beings are often portrayed as helpless, suffering because of the whim of malevolent evil or of a malevolent God.

Scripture dramatises overwhelming nature and gives it religious language and meaning. The central event of the Exodus and the Covenant is preceded by the saga-melodramatic ten plagues. Afraid of the sea, the Hebrew people magnified the ocean monsters, e.g. Behemoth and Leviathan (Job 40). Lions terrorise, prowl, 'seeking whom they might devour', and mangle. Nature, which God had used to destroy sinful humanity in the deluge (Gn.6), seems to go berserk, especially when prefiguring and announcing the second coming of Christ.

The Gospels echo the apocalyptic images of Daniel: 'Then there will be great distress such as, until now, since the world began, there never has been, nor ever will be again' (Matt.24:21). The second letter of Peter offers the symbol of a universal conflagration. This, combined with the beasts of the Book of Revelation 13, has fired the imagination of 'End is nigh' preachers and storytellers. Cinema special effects experts have relished the opportunity for terrifying spectacle.

The '70s saw the peak of popularity of 'disaster' movies, but it is not as if film-makers had not previously responded to an audience desire for vicarious thrills in watching accidents, acts of God, and asking 'What if I…?' and comfortably feeling, 'There, but for the grace of God, go I'. After all, the giant iceberg that sank the unsinkable Titanic shocked the world in 1912. The story was filmed as **Titanic** (U.S. 1953) and **A Night to Remember** (G.B. 1958).

Whether it was the 1969 version of Arthur Hailey's **Airport** that caught popular imagination or not, disaster followed disaster on the screen. Producer Irwin Allen made the most popular: **The Poseidon Adventure** and **Towering Inferno.** Producer Dino de Laurentiis did remakes of films like **Hurricane** and brought that Titan figure of innocence and destruction, and of the Beauty and Beast fable, **King Kong,** to the giant screen.

But it was animal figures who made the most impact on audiences, animals who could embody unexplained malice and whose malevolence could be seen as diabolical. Prior to the '70s, the film most remembered for this kind of terror was Alfred Hitchcock's version of Daphne du Maurier's **The Birds.** Inexplicably but cruelly and relentlessly, the birds attack, terrorise and destroy. Commentators saw the film as a suspense thriller offering a symbol, psychologically effective, of the human condition.

Other films tried to explain why human beings should be so victimised. They tried to uncover the human 'sinfulness' that should bring such revenge from nature. In the '50s, **Them** portrayed giant ants, mutants caused by nuclear tests and the contamination of the environment. This genre has been very popular since — commenting on not only nuclear pollution but chemical poisoning and other conservation issues.

Many of these films had B-budget scripts and styles but were, nevertheless, frightening science fiction stories — for instance, those linked to H. G. Wells' novels, **Food of the Gods, Empire of the Ants.** Australia's giant boar rampaging in the Outback deserts against bizarre kangaroo-shooters and pet-food makers was the loathsome **Razorback.** Contaminated nature pursued human hunters in **Day of the Animals.**

But the underlying sources of the belief in malevolent nature and its manifestations have been studied by psychologists. We are more familiar now with the use of nature symbols in religious mythologies, in poetry and, for individuals as well as for cultures and societies, in the subconscious and in dreams. Animals, both real and imagined (unicorns and bunyips, for instance) lurk, play and rampage through our lives.

Herman Melville's allegorical story of Captain Ahab pursuing Moby Dick, the white whale, portrays a quest, an obsession, a wish to confront and conquer, as well as a death-wish. John Huston attempted a version of **Moby Dick** with Gregory Peck in the '50s.

The most widely seen 'Moby Dick' film is **Jaws.** (The sequels and many imitations generally stayed with plot and scares rather than with the deeper issue of nature confronting humans.) Publicity and memory associate **Jaws** with popular horror. But Steven Spielberg's film offers far more: the menacing evil of the giant shark who is not really seen until mid-film, the shark's eye view of its prey (to John Williams' evocative score), the wanton ravaging and destruction.

The second part of the film has three men alone on a boat, (variations on Ahab), challenged to make a human stand against the evil predator. Robert Shaw is the grizzled Ahab, with grim war memories of circling and devouring sharks; he is destroyed by obsession and shark. Richard Dreyfuss is the technological expert, prepared to confront but thwarted by science. Roy Scheider is the Everyman hero who, in fear, and lacking professional hunting or biology skills, eyes Jaws alone on the sea and destroys him. **Jaws** affirms that we live in a good world which, despite horrors, is not destroyed by an evil principle. ■

CHRISTINE . . . *Stephen King's murderous car corrupts her owner.*

35

Technology of Destruction

The products of human ingenuity
can be exploited,
can turn against their creators.
Machines can be seen
as the scourging hand of God.
They can be monstrous
embodiments of evil.

The power and presence of God have been seen in nature, and its unknown and destructive forces been considered as evil. The Hebrew people also saw God's personal intervention in their history as grace and justice. His loving graciousness was clear. His justice, however, had two facets. The prophets called this time of intervention 'The Day of the Lord'. For those who listened to the message of the prophets and repented, this day was a Day of Salvation. Those who hardened their hearts drew down on themselves the punishment of God.

But the prophets saw that God's punishment was wrought through 'instruments'. The Assyrians who conquered the northern kingdom of Israel in 722-21 BC and destroyed Samaria were seen as 'the hand of God'. But these hands of God were often called 'scourges' and described as evil.

In the last hundred years, with developments in science and technology and in destructive weaponry, we have seen universal scourges. The Third Reich and Hitler himself were quickly seen as antichrists and the hope of a thousand-year Reich a diabolical parody of the book of the Apocalypse. Italian film-maker Lucchino Visconti pictured the corruption in society, particularly in the large arms-merchant families like the Krupps, as the Germanic 'Twilight of the Gods', 'Gotterdämmerung'. His film was called **The Damned** and ended with Helmut Berger, representing the new Nazi power, backed by a conflagration.

It is not too difficult a step to see nuclear power and bombs as malevolent technology. Many recent documentaries have been reassessing the history of the first atomic bomb and the destruction of Hiroshima. **Dr. Strangelove** ended with Moscow destroyed. **Fail Safe** had the U.S. President offering to bomb New York to demonstrate that the accidental bombing of Moscow was not premeditated. American television audiences were shocked in 1983 with the scourge of evil nearer home in **The Day After.**

But it is not the technology itself that is evil. Evil is, of course, in the human heart. The Book of Genesis reminds us, with its stories of human sin, that the temptation succumbed to was that of becoming 'like God'. The phrase 'play God' means that someone controls and manipulates the lives of others, but this meaning has a touch of the blasphemous. God, as Scripture often reminds us (for instance, in the story of the father of the prodigal son) is the one who does *not* 'play God'. God is no controller or manipulator. He is creator, allows us our freedom, offers reconciling grace. The phrase might more appropriately be 'play Devil'.

Film-makers have provided us with a catalogue of this kind of diabolical controller, the best-known being Dr. Frankenstein and his victim-monsters. The contemporary Frankensteins are pictured as creating machine monsters. The Devil-figures, the 'anti-christ' scourges, have taken on a technological face.

In **The Terminator,** former Mr. Universe, Arnold Schwarzennegger, is a cyborg in human form, a complex programmed computer sent by 'time warp' from the future to destroy the mother of the warrior-saviour of the coming post-nuclear age. Relentless, when his human cover is destroyed, he continues to pursue, a diabolical skeletal machine.

In a **Pink Panther** cartoon, a meek little car is filled with a high-powered fuel and is transformed into a mean machine, a sleek, black-browed sports car which roars down the highway, the poor Pink Panther hanging on desperately. It is Dr. Jekyll and Mr. Hyde in automobile form!

Of course, the greatest killer machine is the car. Screenwriters have not been slow in creating diabolical cars. In a thriller called straightforwardly **The Car,** a possessed vehicle terrorises the populace, wreaking havoc and death. A variation on this theme is **Crash** where a driverless, self-propelled car rushes to its destructive destiny. Variations on this theme have included **The Hearse** (self-explanatory) and **Killdozer,** a berserk bulldozer. These films opt generally for thrills for the widest audience.

Horror-master Stephen King was not slow to take up the diabolical car theme. His car is **Christine,** a treacherous car who transforms her gauche owner into as crazed and destructive a being as herself.

The best of these films is Steven Spielberg's **Duel,** as the ordinary citizen (called David Mann) is menaced on the highway by a 'Goliath' tanker (we never see the driver as a person). The duel has enough factual detail to make it a credible symbol of the struggle between good and faceless evil.

The newer machine that science-fiction writers and film-makers see as appropriate for a malevolent technology symbol is, of course, the computer.

A youngster feeds his computer with the texts of Inquisition curses and spells, and it becomes murderously bewitched as **Evilspeak.** Julie Christie is the wife of a computer expert; the jealous computer rapes her and she conceives the machine/child, **Demon Seed.** Synopses might make the films sound ludicrous, but they are produced with sufficient flair to make them genuine horror stories.

Michael Crichton has made films utilising these notions of evil computers: **Westworld,** with computerised holidays and gunslingers, where humans join in the action, including 'High Noon' shootouts; **Looker** where computer fashion models control minds through television commercials; **Runaway** where household appliances turn against their owners. The possibilities are as endless as technological developments seem limitless.

The most terrifying computers are those with the power of nuclear destruction. **War Games** showed how clever teenagers could plug into nuclear programmes and the computers take control. **The Forbin Project** showed humans powerless as the U.S. computer moved beyond human control to battle wits with the U.S.S.R. computer.

The most sinister computer was Arthur C. Clarke's invention in Stanley Kubrick's **2001: A Space Odyssey.** He was Hal, the suavely spoken and agreeably subservient machine (courtesy of Douglas Rains' voice) who gradually took control of the space mission, battling wits and life with the astronauts. It was somewhat disappointing to find him redeemed in the sequel **2010.** After all, there is always something fascinating about villains. It is the attraction of evil, and temptation is, by definition, attractive and alluring.

The machines have power for good and evil. ■

THE DOCTOR AND THE DEVILS . . . *Sauve Doctor Rock (Timothy Dalton) is the evil angel of light in this tale by Dylan Thomas.*

36

Lucifers: Angels of Darkness

Evil is not always recognisably ugly or loathsome.
There is a long tradition
from Lucifer to contemporary angels of light
showing the heart of darkness masked in beauty.

'How did you come to fall from the heavens, Daystar, son of Dawn?' (Is. 14:12). 'The great dragon, the primeval serpent, known as the Devil or Satan, who had deceived all the world, was hurled down to the earth and his angels were hurled down with him.' (Rev. 12:9) 'If anyone says to you then, "Look, here is the Christ" or "He is there", do not believe it; for false Christs and false prophets will arise and produce great signs and portents, enough to deceive even the Chosen, if that were possible. There; I have forewarned you.' (Mt. 24:23-25)

Lucifer means literally, bearer of light.

In the Old Testament, New Testament and eastern mythologies, the Morning Star is a symbol of bright dawn and glory. Its decline was sometimes dramatised as a fall from grace. It was eventually associated with the diabolical enemy, the Satan. A creature of beauty could become something evil, something monstrous.

Jesus warned against wolves in sheep's clothing, against false prophets who would say that he had come, here, there. They would also be able to produce great signs and wonders, persuasive enough to gain disciples for themselves, even from the faithful.

In the early Christian centuries, the Desert Fathers spoke of temptation and the approaches of the Devil as enticement and portrayed devils as beautiful women or handsome men, 'Angels of Light', masking darkness.

Luis Bunuel, a long-time critic of formal religiosity and its hypocrisies, made a short feature, **Simon of the Desert,** about one of the most eccentric saints, Simon Stylites, who stayed on top of a column to avoid temptation. In his ironic and irreverent way, Bunuel suggests that temptation is more liable to beset holy men on pillars and shows its lure in the form of actress Sylvia Pinal.

It was the people of the Middle Ages who created gargoyle images of evil.

St. Ignatius Loyola, a master of spirituality, wrote of the discernment of spirits, criteria for the prayerful man or woman to test whether the 'Angel of Light' was truly from God or an attractive embodiment of temptation.

The device of good and evil strangers has been a dramatic way of portraying this ambiguity.

Biblical epics have used the device of the Lucifer quite ingeniously. One of the more creative features of **The Greatest Story Ever Told** was the casting of Donald Pleasence as Satan for the temptations in the desert scenes. Pleasence can look sinister, but as the Devil he took the appearance of a pilgrim encountering Jesus and attempting to mislead him.

For Zeffirelli's **Jesus of Nazareth,** the screenwriters created a character, the secretary of the Sanhedrin, an inoffensive-looking, unobtrusive-seeming man played by Ian Holm. However, it was he who did the masterminding of the pursuit, arrest and execution of Jesus. A word here, a suggestion there, to officials, to high priests, to Judas — the work of a respectable and conscientious official.

One of the most effective portrayals in a contemporary drama of this kind of Lucifer is singer/actor Sting's character in Dennis Potter's **Brimstone and Treacle.** The title suggests hell in suburbia. And it is. An agreeable-looking, pleasant-mannered young man insinuates himself into a typical London household with dire results. Mouthing piety and greeting-card sentiments, he gains power over a middle-aged couple, reveals their secrets and assaults their daughter, who has lain in coma for several years. Admired as a saint, and miracle worker, he is in fact an incarnation of evil, a personification of malevolence.

Sting does the same in the science-fiction epic **Dune.** While the villainous Harkonnens are generally diseased, bloated and evil, Sting is smooth, fair and evil — the ultimate villain to be fought by the hero, Paul Atreides.

Joseph Conrad wrote 'The Heart of Darkness'. Francis Ford Coppola took Conrad's story and based his outstanding picture of the U.S. experience of the war in Vietnam on it, **Apocalypse Now.** The hero is on a journey to the remote jungles beyond the Vietnamese border to confront a brilliant, decorated military hero, Kurz, played by Marlon Brando. But the hell of war and his own powerful, ambitious drives have turned Kurz into a warlord, surrounded by disciple-natives, ruling them with primitive blood rituals and bleak despair. His final words are 'The horror'. Coppola explores the dark heart of the All-American hero in the apocalyptic inferno of America's failure, jungle war.

This heart of darkness and madness is the subject of Ken Russell's **Crimes of Passion.** Anthony Perkins, in **Psycho** vein, portrays a religious minister who has his own shrine of statues and candles and a self-appointed ministry to save prostitutes, but who has become obsessed by sexuality, and an insane self-loathing that can lead only to violent death.

One of the principal Lucifer figures of the screen is the hypocritical priest or religious, like the bishop who let another man go to prison to cover a manslaughter in **The Silence of Dean Maitland,** or the bizarre Sister Ruth who rebelled against convent life in **Black Narcissus.**

With the growing popularity of religious sects and cult communities, the cult leader has become a powerful Lucifer/antichrist figure.

One of the most powerful of these angelic/diabolic cult-leaders is Peter Fonda's Neil Kirklander in **Split Image.** Walking in an aura of gentleness and peace, speaking like a spiritual father to the youngsters turning their backs on family and world, exhorting them to perfection and spiritual peace and joy, he is nevertheless a controller, a manipulator. He believes his own propaganda and thrives on the adulation of his disciples. But he is revealed as cruel, ruthless in pursuing the success of his cult. Exalted by his followers and revered as more than mere mortal, he is the 'Morning Star' of their lives, but audiences see him as an egotistic angel of darkness.

While the fictional characters exude menace and control their disciples, we know that in reality some cult leaders have been worse. In our times, the real horror of Jim Jones urging his followers to mass suicide (the subject of two American telemovies) is breathtakingly diabolical. ■

THE BRIDE . . . *Sting was a Devil in* Brimstone and Treacle. *As a sinister Dr. Frankenstein he creates a beautiful monster (Jennifer Beals).*

37

Tales of the Dark Side

The powers of evil and their influence on earth
have always been symbolised graphically.
Folklore contains a variety of legends
embodying these powers of evil.
Film-makers have responded
like the storytellers of old.

One of the features of Jewish apocalyptic writing, especially in the later Old Testament books and throughout the New, is the symbol of evil. The influence of thinking from the Persian Empire, derived from Zoroaster, about a source of good and a distinct source of evil in the world, led to figures in art and literature that embodied the evil.

The Book of Daniel with its beasts and Prince of Darkness, the reference to the erecting of a statue of Zeus in the Holy of Holies of the temple in Jerusalem as 'the abomination of desolation' fired imaginations trying to cope with the reality and the enormity of evil. The 12th chapter of the Book of Revelation with its devouring dragon is a vivid example. The first letter of Peter talks of the Devil 'roaming the earth like a lion seeking to devour its prey'.

As Europe emerged out of the Dark Ages into Mediaeval times, along with significant developments in education, the establishment of universities and the profound theological syntheses, went the spread of superstition, fascination with witchcraft and the growth of folklore, derived from the turbulent past, that dealt with fear, violence, death and the inexplicable.

Evil found a face in the contortions and distortions of Gothic statuary, cathedral and palace gargoyles, and in the trials of those accused of witchcraft. Mediaeval and Renaissance church frescoes and paintings have frightening scenes of the Last Judgement and Hell, the torments of the damned and the devil-tormentors.

The legends, poems and tales based on oral traditions popularised symbols of evil — the dragon reappeared as the foe of the knight, St. George. Slaying dragons was a feature of chivalric lore.

Madness, the moon and the baying of predatory wolves stimulated the imagining of wolf-men and -women, symbols of the beast within the human being. Passed down through generations, they survive in seemingly playful nursery rhymes and fairy tales like Little Red Riding Hood.

Early in the history of 20th century cinema, these old legends were taken up by film-makers. They expressed both the artist's insights into human nature and the sense that audiences would respond via the new medium in the way that listeners to spoken tales responded through the centuries: with fascination and terror.

Nightmares could be an essential part of celluloid dreams, sometimes exploiting the terror of the audience, sometimes bringing evil symbolically before people who would like to deny it or hide it.

It is interesting that the first major horror films came from the post-World War I German film industry, with its expressionist style, silent screen icons of vampires, the living dead, murderous somnambulists and mastermind criminals (**Nosferatu, Golem, Cabinet of Caligari, Dr. Mabuse**).

While most film industries have some horror stories in their repertoire, it was the U.S. industry that took up the German lead of the '20s. In the early '30s came two features that have extensively influenced 20th century images: **Frankenstein** and **Dracula.** During the '30s, the Hollywood studios turned out a large number of variations on these themes. This trend continued into the '40s but what frightened and intrigued Depression audiences seemed distant from the actual horrors of World War II. Many of the horror films of the '40s were spoofs.

Again there was a lull until, in the late '50s, the British film industry at Hammer Studios started to remake the '30s classics in colour and with more explicit violence. They continued remaking them for almost 20 years. The result was a mixture of 'good fun' and 'creepiness'.

In the United States in 1978, a small-budget horror film by John Carpenter about madness, multiple murders and a seemingly indestructible wielder of vengeance, **Halloween,** found itself a cult movie. It was imitated and re-imitated in a glut of derivative horror.

By the '80s, most industries were churning out horror films, many of which were exercises in gore and nastiness, and many serious attempts at continuing the legends were lost in the welter of box-office exploitation. But the film experience tells us that, in our own way, no matter what our sophistication, the symbols of evil still speak to us.

The main symbols of evil, of the Devil or demons, in these films were:
- Dracula — Nosferatu; the Mediaeval Transylvanian tyrant, Vlad, whose cruelty was legend, who died but roamed the earth by night seeking the blood of the pure.
- The Living Dead — Variations on the vampire theme, local cultures having their particular characters and stories like the Jewish Golem, the Caribbean zombies, the Egyptian mummies.
- Frankenstein — Dr. Frankenstein was an arrogant man who abused science to 'play God' and by use of criminal brains created destructive monsters. He is fellow to many 'Mad Doctors' like Dr. Phibes.
- Wolfman/Werewolves — Often the most sympathetic symbol, since many wolf-men and -women were innocent victims transformed and killed; variations include Beauty and the Beast tales. Mr. Hyde is the wolf-man in Dr. Jekyll.
- Avengers — In the tradition of the Apocalyptic avenging angels, rooting

out and destroying evil, stories ranging from Jack the Ripper tales to the modern urban vigilante.

Naturally, these stories, like their many predecessors over the centuries, were not always welcomed by many sections of society. Yet they have persisted and, in ages where respectability has been pursued at the expense of honesty, the stories have surfaced. One wonders why Mary Shelley's 'Frankenstein', Bram Stoker's 'Dracula' and Robert Louis Stevenson's 'Dr. Jekyll and Mr. Hyde' all emerged from 19th century England. It seems tales of the dark side, nightmares, are always necessary. ■

MEPHISTO . . . *Klaus Maria Brandauer, powerful as the actor Hendrik Hofgen, who sells his soul to the Third Reich. Directed by Istvan Szabo.*

38

Allegorical and Satirical Devils

In order to cope
with the reality of evil and sinfulness in the world
(and in each individual),
artists have created figures
who clearly embody antichrist qualities.
They can be serious figures
or satiric figures of fun.

Allegory has been a favourite figure of speech for preachers and moralists for centuries. The metaphor appeals to the imagination. But, just in case the audience is not as alert as it might be, the allegory-maker makes quite clear the parallels between characters and incidents in the story and their counterparts in real life. The representations in the allegory are for some didactic purpose, often moral.

The Old Testament book of Daniel and the New Testament Apocalypse contain prominent scriptural allegories. The statue of various metals but clay feet that topples represents a succession of identifiable ancient kingdoms; so too does the beast with multiple horns.

This kind of language and vision is taken up at the end of the New Testament period in the allegories of John's Book of Revelation. The examples suggested are of evil kingdoms. While there are allegories of light and goodness, a dramatic way of presenting evil is by personification and allegory.

One might ask what idols are, and hear the answer that, basically, they are allegorical character-representations of qualities of good and evil. Humankind has been idol-making from the beginning — Adam and Eve setting themselves up in the garden 'to be like God'. In fact, this temptation to 'play God' has been evident throughout the centuries, as tyrants from Nero to Hitler have set themselves up as diabolical idols. We see them as symbols of evil; their cruel lives make them appear as allegorical devils.

This can be taken to frightening, as well as ludicrous, extremes. The history of Satanism and witchcraft, of the occult and of cults of Satan reminds us that humans are fascinated by their shadow side and have submitted themselves to and worshipped their devil, antichrist figures.

In the '70s and '80s, many films have played on this behaviour, capitalising on tantalising advertisements and box office hopes with bizarre plots, special effects and going over the top in absurd cult behaviour: titles like **Spectre, Satanic Rites of Dracula, Ghoulies, Blood from the Mummy's Tomb.**

If these allegorical devils are set up as idols to be toppled seriously, or as figures of fun, they are satirical. We remember that the satirist mocks idols and idolators. The satirist, as a savage moralist, may be angry at the ridiculous, inwardly yearning for authentic values.

An entertaining example of this kind of satirical, allegorical devil is Stanley Donen's **Bedazzled,** with Peter Cook and Dudley Moore. It is a modern morality play with Dudley Moore as Stanley, a '60s London Everyman who is prepared to sell his soul to the Devil to be with his beloved. He has seven wishes, which send up British society at all levels and show how the Seven Deadly Sins have penetrated the world. Peter Cook is George Spigot, alias the Devil.

The screenplay shows George wreaking mischief and havoc but also nastily spoiling Stanley's wishes and, in fact, exploiting those wishes and winning literally every trick. Peter Cook makes a feasible suave, callous, lying modern Devil.

Ingmar Bergman also has his mock-devil. In **The Devil's Eye,** Satan wants victims for hell, particularly those who are chaste. He sends Don Juan up to earth on a seduction mission because, as a proverb goes, a chaste woman is a sty in the Devil's eye.

The Devil or his minion, especially Mephistopheles, features allegorically to significant advantage in the many versions of the Dr. Faustus legend. Great artists like Christopher Marlowe, Goethe, Gounod and Klaus Mann have portrayed Faust wanting knowledge and power, selling his soul to the Devil. The antichrist choice of eternal damnation prevails over salvation for the bliss of a short game.

There have been film versions, for example, of Marlowe's play with Richard Burton. Creative variations have included Brian de Palma's rock musical **Phantom of the Paradise,** where a composer buys other people's talent and a Dorian Grey-like youthfulness, or the powerful film version of Klaus Mann's **Mephisto** where Karl Maria Brandauer plays a German actor who sells himself to the Nazis to play greater stage and screen roles. Ironically, his best role is that of Goethe's Mephisto.

The Faust story can be translated into any situation because we are all prey to temptation, liable to be seduced by a wily demon to sell our selves, even if only a fragmentary part, for what we can never get by ourselves.

A well-known variation of the Faust legend from English literature is Oscar Wilde's 'The Picture of Dorian Grey'.

One of the best-known practitioners of allegorical antichrist figures was Ian Fleming. In his James Bond stories, he has a succession of villains who represent evil, the Devil and sin, especially the seven deadly sins. The film versions of the novels (at least after the first four in the early '60s) resembled the books generally in title and character names only — though, with their larger-than-life villains played by strong character actors, they are cinema comic-book versions of what Fleming had in mind.

Fleming's interest in the seven deadly sins and his villains is evident from the discussion about good and evil in his first Bond novel 'Casino Royale'. Obviously Goldfinger is Greed, the ultimate villain; Blofeld gets as close to any allegorical figure of a devil who has gained a whole world and experienced absolute soullessness. Fleming's books (and to a much less explicit extent, the films) show that moralistic fables can still reach the widest audience through the entertainment forms of the day.

A postscript on the deadly sins is the amusing film, **The Chain,** in which seven people move house in London (mostly upwardly mobile) on the one day. The satiric point is that each represents one of the seven deadly sins. Nigel Hawthorne's upper middle class avarice, for instance, shows that allegoric sin-devil-figures need not be presented on any cosmic scale.

In the suburbs will do. ■

ALAMO BAY . . . *Human malevolence in the form of the Ku Klux Klan sails against Vietnamese refugees.*

39

Malice without Motive

Malevolence is the wishing of evil on another.
While the world and its human development
seem malevolent,
there is in the heart of individuals
and, thus, of society,
a malice that seems malign,
without motive.
It is diabolical.

We live in a world pervaded by evil.

We live in a world of God's creative and loving graciousness, but we are constantly aware of pervasive evil. There is a mystery of evil in the human heart, the heart's capacity for willing harm and destruction on others, for self-seeking and for self-seeking at the expense of others. As human beings we can be benevolent, wishing well to others; but we can be malevolent, wishing ill to others.

Another word to describe these evil attitudes and behaviour is 'malice'. Shakespeare has created many frighteningly evil villains, like Richard the Third. But Othello's friend and confidant Iago must be one of the most malicious of human beings. Commentators have spoken of his 'motiveless malignity', a consuming malice that eats away Iago's soul as he contrives Othello's downfall. Shakespeare uses devil imagery to denote this malice. Iago is human but he is seen to have a cloven foot; a sinister, diabolical destroyer.

The character of malice is often a striking antichrist figure.

Paul was aware of this capacity for malice, the inner evil that, despite his desire not to do it, nevertheless drove him on to 'the evil that he did not want to do'.

The Gospels present Jesus' reflections:

For it is from within, from men's hearts, that evil intentions emerge: fornication, theft, murder, adultery, avarice, malice, deceit, indecency, envy, slander, pride, folly. All these evil things come from within and make a man unclean. (Mark 7:21-23).

Jesus himself was the victim of this kind of malice. A glance at the gallery of Jesus' enemies, their motives and the way they treated him, makes a powerful story of malevolence: the Pharisees with their self-righteous jealousy, the Sadducees with their contemptuous dismissal of his message, the High Priests, Annas and Caiaphas, who proclaimed it better for one man to die for the good of the nation, Herod and his disappointed mockery, the fickle and jeering crowds who preferred Barabbas, the condemnation by Pilate, unable to overcome his fear, the insulting thief and, of course, Judas, of whom John says that the Devil entered into his heart — 'and it was night' (John 13:30).

Some film-writers and directors have been fascinated by this inner malice and the consequences for others. They have often chosen the horror and science-fiction genres to symbolise this evil. For instance, Canadian David Cronenberg has made several features that comment on society and its sick individuals who spread their malice like a contagion.

The conventions of the horror film are used to often gruesome effect — which puts his films outside the range of ordinary film-goers.

His symbols have included gross internal parasites or growths that infect others (**Shivers, Rabid**), creatures that are physical embodiments of inner evil produced unconsciously by individuals (**The Brood**) or technological evil in deadly weapons that can explode other people (**Scanners**). In **Videodrome,** a cable television channel featuring 'Snuff Movies', films of actual killings, literally takes hold and grips individuals and destroys them. Strong stuff, but powerful images.

Science-fiction turned psychological science-fantasy has sometimes taken the theme of human beings projecting their inner evil into destructive creatures. A popular fantasy of the '50s, **Forbidden Planet,** a science-fiction variation on Shakespeare's **The Tempest,** showed a civilisation that had destroyed itself by such evil becoming manifest, and Walter Pidgeon's Dr. Morbius/Prospero was unwittingly doing the same in his arrogance.

The same happened in a small-budget '80s film, **Galaxy of Terror,** where the members of the space team were destroyed by their own evil images. In **The Keep,** in the Carpathian Mountains during World War II, a diabolical creature kept trying to make itself more human and had to be contained within the castle keep. These were effective cinema symbols of malevolence.

Like Iago, some characters in films display for us 'motiveless malignity'. It can be on a domestic level, a malicious child in **The Bad Seed,** or a ruthlessly selfish individual like those played (and seen on TV late shows) by Bette Davis. One of the best of these is in John Huston's **In This Our Life,** a woman bent on controlling and hurting everyone, but ultimately in a hell of her own making.

Whatever the historical reality of the lives of Mozart and Salieri, the play and film version of Peter Shaffer's **Amadeus** offer an extraordinary character in Maestro Salieri. F. Murray Abraham's Oscar-winning performance as Salieri portrays a character consumed by ambition, envy and anger, a mediocrity in his field who endures the hell of fully appreciating the beauty of Mozart's music but who has no capacity for emulating it.

Initially a devout young man, he turns against the God he trusted and withdraws into his own insane world where he is both Mozart's genius (in collaborating with his 'Requiem') and destroyer (in believing that he had murdered him). A powerful depiction of malice.

On a grander scale, a genre of films showing malice is the gangster movie. The Scarfaces, Little Caesars and Public Enemies of the '30s drew on the

Prohibition thugs like Al Capone who controlled crooked kingdoms. In the '70s and '80s, the gangster film reached its peak with Francis Ford Coppola's **Godfather** films and Sergio Leone's epic **Once Upon A Time In America.** Here the empires of evil were displayed.

While the stories caught up their audiences in their plots and characterisations, they also left them in dismay at insidious and rampant evil. Don Corleone was evil, but the corruption, decline and fall of his son, Michael, was a horrifying example of contemporary malice — parallelled as it was by the intercutting of baptismal scenes (the Godfather of faith) and massacres (Godfather of death).

The conspiracy of evil on a worldwide scale, the intricacies and tangles of power and greed webs, is seen to best effect in the thriller novels of writers like Robert Ludlum. Unfortunately, the few film versions, **The Osterman Weekend, The Holcroft Covenant,** have not pictured or communicated their world with the power of the books.

A final image of malice controlling the world comes from the imagination of Ira Levin (who also imagined the incarnation of Satan as **Rosemary's Baby**). In **The Boys From Brazil,** he has sadistic concentration camp doctor and experimenter, Josef Mengele (Gregory Peck), continuing his work from his hideaway refuge in South America: the genetic cloning of Hitler. Mengele has succeeded in placing his 'Hitler boys' throughout the world, awaiting the second coming of the 20th century's most powerful embodiment of evil. It is ironic that Mengele fears dogs and is ultimately savaged to death by large black hellhounds, hounded to death by his fears.

Malice consumes the soul and destroys itself. ■

AGNES OF GOD . . . *Is Agnes Christ-like? Is she naive, mad, a victim, a saint? Meg Tilly as Agnes, with Jane Fonda as her court-appointed psychiatrist.*

40

Film: in Search of Meaning

As has been seen, cinema is considered the art form of the 20th century. It has undergone significant changes during the century in both form and content: sound, colour, wide screen processes, experiments with developing technology as well as simple storytelling, documenting of events, comedy, musical, western, science-fiction, drama. It has been seen as the art for popular entertainment. It has been used as a moralising and didactic art. It has been the vehicle for films that have mirrored the world and have depthed it.

Films have represented humanity and interpreted it.

Films have also become more accessible. Television preserves many of them for a new life and a new audience. Video availability puts them literally into our hands.

This is a responsibility. Individuals read books — and individuals watch films. But watching a film in a limited time and space and generally with others means shared experience. This book has attempted to point to ways of seeing films. It has not advocated a 'reading into films' what is not there, what exists only in the imagination of the beholder. Rather, it has indicated some ways of seeing more clearly and accurately what is there, alerting us to the clues, the indicators, the references which enable us to evaluate more fully what the makers have put into the film.

We do this for most arts; we train students to appreciate them. We have been remiss with training for the art that appeals to the widest audience.

This is a pity because films open up the world of values. As audiences identify with or reject identification with characters, their sensitivity, empathy and ethical and moral stances can be drawn on. What can easily be labelled as 'immoral' on the level of reason and argumentation takes on a different dimension when seen in the complexity of characters in dilemma situations. Compassion is necessary as well as clear-sightedness and principles.

Twentieth century psychology has alerted us to the differing ways in which we perceive the world and the differing ways in which we go into action. C. G. Jung, for instance, notes that some (most?) people perceive the world in its detail, facts and order, while others (absent-minded?) tend to overlook detail but 'pick up the vibes'. Neither is right nor wrong.

Obviously, they can be of mutual benefit, one extending the range of the other. The same with decision-making: some rely on logic, others on their more subjective assessment of a situation. Again, neither right nor wrong. Again, complementary.

This means that response to films can be rich and varied. We are always able to discover more. With the different genres of storytelling and the conventions that go with the genres, we have representations of good and evil that are not merely factual but symbolic. We are invited into a world of meaning.

Our focus has been on the representations of Jesus, of those who resemble Jesus and those who are the opposite of Jesus.

The portrayals of Jesus himself on screen, the cinema Jesus-figures, have not been numerous. What has happened is a change from a pious representation that is considered 'realistic' to a more stylised representation, sometimes relying more on recent art styles than on those more generally accepted or traditional. But, despite some hopes to the contrary in the early '70s, even the phrase 'Jesus Christ Superstar' has become accepted.

The Christ-figure is wide-ranging. The significant, substantial resemblance to Jesus is essential. But, since it is a 'figure' of Jesus, we should not be too surprised if the Christ-figure is a mix of good and evil. Paul said this of himself — but did not hesitate to stake his claim as a Christ-figure and urge us to imitate him.

Jesus is both suffering redeemer and risen saviour. Christ-figures resemble him as both redeemer and saviour. In the turbulence of recent decades, a new name has been found for the redeemer-saviour: for so many peoples experiencing oppression, who long for and struggle for a new Exodus, Jesus is *liberator.*

Part of the excitement of discovering a Christ-figure is identifying the resemblance to Jesus. Also part of the excitement is breaking through categories, helpful as they are, to new appreciations of Jesus himself in the light of the Christ-figure. Jesus himself is revealed anew through the Christ-figure.

Even from the earliest decades of the Church's life, there have been alternative Saviour-figures. And there has been malice — from inside the human heart, as well as outside in the evil that the malicious heart contrives. From early stories where the serpent in Eden was anti-God, the opposition between good and evil is the classic human story.

The opposition to Christ in both its serious and its absurd manifestations posits an antichrist, a particular form of the confrontation of good by evil. The antichrist figure, therefore, takes its place over against the Christ-figures.

In every age there have been attempts by sincere and zealous members of the Church to proclaim their faith, explain it, defend it; attempts to make it credible to those who do not share it. In our secular age, where formal religion has less power, but the search for values is still of supreme importance, the Christ-figure (as well as the antichrist figure) may be an interesting, arresting and credible way to dialogue about the significance of Jesus and his Good News.

The recent film version of John Piehlmeier's play **Agnes of God** screened to mixed reactions: strange happenings in an enclosed convent, dotty nuns or, on the other hand, the clash between faith and reason and the possibility of victimised innocence. Sister Agnes of God (Agnus Dei — Lamb of God) is a Christ-figure, humiliated and brutalised by her mother, hysteric in her manifestations of holiness (stigmata, perhaps her pregnancy) but, nevertheless, a person of beauty and guilelessness who encourages the Superior in her faith and makes the lapsed Catholic psychologist realise that she has been touched by goodness ... ■

THE MISSION . . . *As in* The Name of the Rose, *the Church figures presented by* The Mission, *starring Robert De Niro and Jeremy Irons, vary greatly regarding their resemblance to Christ.*

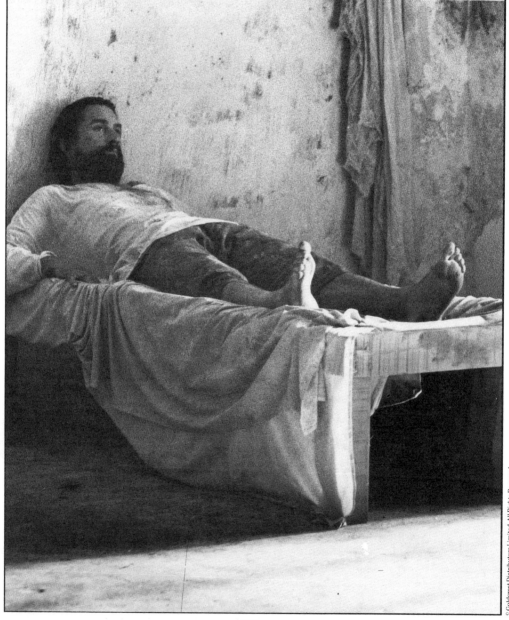

41

An Approach to Interpretation

It is not usually possible to find Jesus-figures, Christ-figures and antichrist figures all in one film. However, they are all present in the film version of Umberto Eco's novel, **The Name of the Rose.** It provides a useful example to focus the themes of this book.

Eco wrote of a Church in spiritual and theological decline in 1327. The plot unfolds in a Benedictine monastery in remote northern Italy, where a theological debate is to be held on the question, 'Did Jesus own his own clothes?'. Behind the dubious verbal sparring is a Franciscan challenge to ecclesiastical wealth and worldliness, and the presence of a torturing Inquisition hounding heretics belonging to fanatic, apocalyptic fringe-groups. Simultaneously, within the monastery, monks are being killed, and Friar William of Baskerville (Sean Connery as an urbane mediaeval Sherlock Holmes) investigates the mystery.

The Name of the Rose explores verbal Jesus-figures. There is much talk of whether Jesus owned his own tunic — a Gospel Jesus of unworldly poverty. A key issue is a dispute about the personality of Jesus — whether he laughed or not. The more humane protagonists see a smiling, even a laughing Jesus. The stern ascetics say Jesus never laughed, and therefore, his disciples should not either. Laughter casts out fear, and without fear, there would be a lessening of Church authority.

An alert audience is challenged to reflect on its own Jesus-figures.

With so many monks in the monastery, as well as visiting Franciscans, there is great potential for Christ-figures. However, most of the clerics are presented as grotesque, even physically. The mediaeval religious do not offer much of an authentic face of Christ.

William of Baskerville and his young novice companion (the narrator in the novel) present a better image. William, who had himself previously risked compromise in serving the tyrannical Inquisition, feels somehow responsible for the deaths of the seemingly innocent victims of the unknown murderer. But in the monastery, and in the eyes of the novice, Adso, he appears as a man of prayer, insight, and wisdom, dealing fairly with monks, Inquisitors, judges and oppressed villagers.

His humanitarian spirituality, a blend of Gospel values and perceptions — and, in particular, of Christ-like forgiveness and understanding of his confused novice — has the dimensions of a Christ-figure. Adso himself, infatuated with a village girl and moved to pity for her, is zealous to save her from the Inquisitor's fire. They are both, each in his own way, attractive and gentle 'saviours'.

The Middle Ages exhibited a superstitious fascination with the Devil, and with magic and witchcraft. Ignorant men and women, caught up in wild interpretations of the Apocalypse, practised black magic rituals with cats, cocks, and potions, evocations of evil. In Eco's plot, the antichrist figures of malevolence abound, from the self-righteous murdering monk who fears the power of laughter, to the arrogant Grand Inquisitor, executing hapless victims in the name of a 'divine right' to rule the Church.

The Name of the Rose can be seen as gathering up the best of the features of the Christ-figures and the worst of the antichrists.

CONCLUDING COMMENTS

- Not every film offers Christ-figures.
- However, viewers can develop an alertness to characters who can be discerned as 'redeeming' their fellow human beings, self-sacrificing characters, or 'saving' characters who empower and enable others to transcend themselves. Thus a capacity can be developed to recognise qualities in characters that might be otherwise overlooked, and so enhance understanding and appreciation at a deeper level.
- Film stories with age-old plots that dramatise the conflict between good and evil are obvious opportunities for sharpening our sensitivity towards Christ-figures. These stories can range from contemporary popular myth-making to the struggles in families or in society that have been the stuff of classic drama in every age.
- After seeing a film, we may realise that we have identified strongly with a particular character. Checking out the reasons for identifying with, or, on the other hand, being repelled by another character, might be a further way of depthing the quality of our film-viewing.
- Comparing notes is always a stimulating way to develop our capacity to respond. The delight of sharing viewpoints can be a welcome and encouraging reassurance. The salutary shock of encountering someone else's differing interpretation or reaction can help to broaden our own perspectives.
- Of course, as this book has been at pains to point out, a character who is genuinely a Christ-figure resembles Jesus substantially and significantly; otherwise, we empty the phrase (and the idea itself) of meaning. Again, the indications must come from the film itself — not from our reading into films, or projecting on to them a pious interpretation.
- But searching out the cinematic Christ-figures can be a fruitful way of appreciating films, their values and their layers of meaning.

Some of the questions suggested below may be of assistance in this task. However, note that they are intended as discussion-starters, and are not designed to make film-viewers impose the notion of Christ-figure where there is none.

WHEN YOU NEXT SEE A FILM THAT ARRESTS YOUR ATTENTION AND RAISES QUESTIONS ABOUT VALUES, TRY ASKING YOURSELF:

1. What was the main point of interest for you in this film: a character? the plot? the dialogue? the setting? something else?...

2. In reflecting on your response to the film, which sequences do you think best presented the main point of interest?

3. Could you identify with the character(s) who dramatised the theme? Or were you repelled by some character(s)?

4. Did the film seem to you to show a conflict between good and evil? Which characters represented the good, and which the evil?

5. How much did the hero and/or heroine seem to you to represent the good? Or was this the role of a significant supporting character?

6. Did the 'good' character enable others to change, or to be their 'better' selves?

7. If your answer was 'yes', how did the 'good' character achieve this change — by some self-sacrificing attitudes and behaviour (i.e. as a 'redeemer-figure') or by leading others beyond themselves to peace, happiness or love (i.e. as a 'saviour-figure')?

8. How did the redeemer-figure(s) or saviour-figure(s) resemble the Gospel portrait of Jesus Christ? Did you notice incidents and behaviour in the film which seemed to mirror Gospel incidents?

9. Did these resemblances enable you to perceive the 'Christ-qualities' of the character(s)? Has this reflection brought about any change in your own perception of the Jesus of the Gospels (your 'Jesus-figure')?

10. How did the characters who represented evil depict anti-God, antichrist attitudes familiar from Scripture? Explicitly? Implicitly?

11. What insights into evil and its workings did these antichrist figures give you?

12. In what ways did this exploration of Christ-figures (and antichrists) enhance your response to the film?

INDEX OF FILM TITLES